STUPIDITY
IS NOT A GIFT OF GOD

 OREST STOCCO

STUPIDITY IS NOT A GIFT OF GOD

Spiritual Musings - Volume 3

Copyright © 2013 by OREST STOCCO

All rights reserved. No part of this book may be reproduced or transmitted in any form or by any means without written permission of the author.

ISBN 978-0-9920112-3-9

Edited by Penny Lynn Cates

Cover Design by Penny Lynn Cates

Table of Contents

Prologue

PART ONE

1. The Ozymandian Factor 1
2. Quantum Spirituality Post 2012 6
3. The Miracle of the Individuation Process 10
4. Deus Ex Machina 15
5. The Riddle of Atheism 20
6. Healing the Soul of the World One Soul at a Time......24
7. The Co-existence of Parallel Worlds............................26
8. My Journey to Authenticity 30
9. Chance or Divine Intervention?....................................33
10. Prisoners of Our Own Vanity 40
11. Trust God, but Don't Forget To Flush the Toilet..........47
12. Is Jesus Christ Relevant Today.....................................50
13. A Very Strange Virus 54
14. Who's Driving Your Bus Today? 60
15. The Gnostic Wisdom of Life 67
16. The Wasteland of the Soul 71
17. The Secret Way of Life 74
18. The Gurdjieff Fallacy 79
19. The Process of Life...84
20. The Fear of Self-knowledge 89
21. Good Lives Well Lived Are Heroic 95

22. The Mystical Power of Story	100
23. 10,000 Hours, Past Lives, or Luck of the Draw	107
24. Life after Life	113
25. The Special Message of Story	117
26. A Bee in My Window	121
27. The Conversion Experience	126
28. A Cheap Shot at Shirley MacLaine	131
29. An Exercise in Active Imagination	137
30. The Perennial Philosophy	147
31. Our Sacred Contract	152
32. A Window on the Soul of Man	156
33. The Omniscient Guiding Force and Vicissitudes of Life	160
34. Stupidity Is Not a Gift of God	164
35. Life Only Makes Sense When We Know Why We Are Here	170
Epilogue	175
Insights: A Personal Essay	178
The Making of a Novel: Tea with Grace	187
An Interview With The Author	189

Prologue

Books have their own soul. Every writer knows this. And books choose their own title. They may choose their title before the book is written, very much like the soul of an unborn child may come to the mother in a dream and announce what name he or she wishes to be called when they are born, or it may announce its name while the book is being written, or after it has been birthed; such is the mystery of book writing.

Although my title came to me long before I wrote the first musing, I agonized for months whether I should call this third volume of spiritual musings *Stupidity Is Not a Gift of God*, because it smacked of such intellectual hubris that I felt it was sure to throw most readers off once they got over the initial humorous first impression, and I discarded the title half a dozen times in my mind before it finally won me over.

Actually, when it announced itself to me it came with a dual name, like my second volume of spiritual musings, *Old Whore Life, Exploring the Shadow Side of Karma*. In a very proud, though not boastful voice the soul of my new book revealed its identity: *Stupidity Is Not a Gift of God, It's Entirely Man-made;* but for reasons inspired by Hemingway's iceberg theory of writing, I did not include the second part of the title in the belief that my reader would realize that it was implied in my spiritual musings. But however much trust I placed in my reader, my Muse insisted that I write a prologue just in case the title left a lingering bad taste in the reader's mouth.

In all honesty, I felt sick to my stomach when I was struck by the outrageous hubris of my book's title, because it suggested a divine intelligence that I did not possess; and only after it revealed its essential nature to me did I see the aesthetic value of my title, thereby affirming what the writer Karen Blixen (*Out of Africa*) said about the creative process: **"Art is the truth above the facts of life."**

In some circles of life it is believed that the name is the thing, reflecting the Platonic theory that archetypal forms are the essential nature of their expressed reality; so did the soul of my title reveal its essential nature to me with each new spiritual musing that I wrote, and only upon completing my twenty-ninth musing ("An Exercise in Active Imagination") did I feel confident enough to embrace my cheeky title without misgivings.

What, then, is the aesthetic truth of *Stupidity Is Not a Gift of God*? What was the soul of my new book of spiritual musings trying to tell me by calling itself this name?

As I wrote in my forward "A Word for My Reader" in my second volume of spiritual musings, "My spiritual musings are a form of creative self-reflection," and I came to see that the aesthetic truth of *Stupidity Is Not a Gift of God* is the simple truth that we write the script of our own life; and when tragedy befalls us, we have no one to blame but the author of our own life script—but seldom do we hold ourselves accountable; ergo, *stupidity is not a gift of God, it's entirely man-made!*

My Muse knew this aesthetic truth, but I had to work it out in the writing of my book; and that's the mystery of creative writing. A book gives birth to its own reality, its own truth. But as I said, sometimes the soul of a book announces its name before the book is written, and sometimes during or after it has been written; it all depends upon the author's relationship with his Muse, and by Muse I mean the creative unconscious whose sole purpose seems to be, as I have come to understand it, to make conscious the unconscious through the divine miracle of the creative process.

In my first book *What Would I Say Today If I Were to Die Tomorrow?* I wrote, **"Self-deception is our greatest threat to personal growth, happiness, and wholeness."** I've written ten books since, and with each new book that I wrote the aesthetic truth of my first book continued to hold true. In fact, it was re-enforced with each new book that I wrote; which only makes me smile more sweetly at the epigraph that I used to introduce my first book: *"As you grow older in your observations of the peoples of this Earth world, it becomes more noticeable that stupidity is the reigning virtue."*

But why? Why must we continue to blunder our way through the calamitous misfortunes of our own stupidities? Why, indeed?

This has preoccupied writers for centuries, from the tragedies of Sophocles to the plays of Shakespeare and contemporary writers like John Irving—"We are formed by what we desire. In less than a minute of excited, secretive longing I desired to become a writer and have sex with Miss Frost—not necessarily in that order" (from Irving's *In One Person,* a novel of conflicted sexuality); and it will continue to preoccupy us until we resolve the paradoxical ontology of our nature, which is always a personal responsibility.

Stupidity Is Not a Gift of God then is another creative effort to come to terms with who we are; and if it smacks of hubris, so be it.

PART ONE

*"The most dangerous person ever to deceive is yourself,
for in doing so you destroy your basis for honesty.
Honesty is the foundation of intelligence,
while dishonesty is the foundation
of stupidity."*

LOVE WITHOUT END, JESUS SPEAKS
Glenda Green

1. The Ozymandian Factor

It all started with something that Jesus said in Glenda Green's book that I was reading with my morning coffee: ***"You do not have to seek your lessons. They find you. Too often people seek a lesson or purpose elsewhere because they think the one in front of them is not good enough. Often they are hard on themselves by seeking difficult lessons while failing to respect the power of the simple lesson staring them in the face. You have quite enough before you. When you have mastered that, your next lesson will appear"*** (*Love without End, Jesus Speaks*, p. 91). That hit so close to home I had to stop reading.

My lesson was staring me in the face. I had to assemble all my notes for the new book that I was writing on living my same life over again in a parallel world (my working title is *The Summoning of Noman, The True Story of My Parallel Life,* a reference to the anonymous medieval English morality play *The Summoning of Everyman*), but I procrastinated and went on the Internet to explore *Lilou's Juicy Living Tour.*

I checked out her list of interviews and came upon Gary Zukav again, whom I kept avoiding because something about him bothered me. I also kept putting off her interview with Dr. Wayne Dyer because something about him bothered me also; but I suspected I was projecting, and it was time to face that aspect of my shadow personality.

I had read *The Seat of the Soul* when it came out a number of years ago, which got Gary Zukav onto the Oprah Winfrey show and catapulted his career, and I didn't know if it was shadow envy of his literary success that kept me from reading any more of his books and watching the interview with Lilou Mace, but I felt it was time to find out...

As much as I hate to admit this, somewhere in my journey to authenticity I began to sense a certain *je ne sais quoi* about some successful people that annoyed me, like the singer Ann Murray; whenever I heard her singing I got the creepy feeling that her shadow had become her reality, and it gave me the willies. It was like the false had become the real in the same way that movie actors say, *"When you can fake the real you've got it made."* Or like Thomas Hudson said about his deck hand Peters in Hemingway's novel *Islands in the Stream*: "He is like the false carried so far it has been made true." That's the only way I can describe how Ann Murray's voice affected me, and it made me uncomfortable.

Dubbed "the lugubrious warbler" by Shinan Govani of the *National Post*, Canadian singer Rufus Wainwright also gave me the willies. His singing never failed to create the impression that he was stuck in the seventh level of hell, as though the vibrations of his voice spoke to where he was at on his spiritual journey through life. Neil Young also, whose voice sounded to me like a tortured blend of squealing and whining; and the iconic singer-poet Leonard Cohen, whom I dubbed "the guru of angst" because he can't seem to get off his treadmill of despair—*"Dressed in black with short cropped hair, /He milks the udder of despair. /A poet, singer, lover, and thief /He churns the sour milk of life into pure gold /And lives like a lavish prince..."* I wrote in a poem that he inspired years ago; but that's precisely why these singers are so popular—because they resonate with anyone that is stuck on their own treadmill of despair, which includes a very large spectrum of society.

Misery loves company. But with Gary Zukav and Dr. Wayne Dyer it was different. To borrow a phrase from Connie Zweig (*Romancing the Shadow*), they have "romanced their shadow" and are cashing in on the confrontation with their unconscious self by sharing their personal journey to authenticity with the world; but there was still something of that elusive "it" factor about them that bothered me, and I feared that it spoke to my shadow personality. That's why I had to watch Lilou's interview with Gary Zukav.

I watched and listened very carefully, trying not to be judgmental because I wanted to give him the benefit of the doubt; and although I felt that he had come a long way on his journey to authenticity since he wrote *The Seat of the Soul,* it was obvious to me that he still had a long way to go to resolve the stubborn last vestiges of that irritating "it" factor that I recognized instantly as the conceit of his personal journey to authenticity—what Gurdjieff would have mercilessly called the "chief feature" of our "false personality."

Once I saw the proud face of his shadow personality—that same archetypal spirit of vanity that St. Padre Pio slew in me with the devastating power of redemptive love during my spiritual healing sessions that became the basis of my novel *Healing with Padre Pio*—Zukav said something that confirmed his conceit; and that's when my Muse gave me the title for a new spiritual musing ("Trust God, but Don't Forget to Flush the Toilet"), which distilled the wisdom of Zukav's quest for authenticity with aphoristic clarity—

"You have to align your personality with your soul," Zukav said to Lilou, revealing the ancient secret of the Way that speaks to the paradoxical mystery of man's personal karmic destiny and pre-ordained spiritual destiny; but not until the two destinies become one as Jesus tells us will we be made whole: "For when the master himself was asked by someone when his kingdom would come, he said, **'When the two will be one, and the outer like the inner, and the male with the female neither male nor female,"** (*The Unknown Sayings of Jesus*, Marvin Meyer, p. 95).

That was his challenge still. It's ironic then that Gary Zukav, whom I kept avoiding all these years, should be the inspiration for my third volume of spiritual musings. I could see that he was still in the throes of becoming his authentic self and that I was no longer projecting, and I knew from confronting the vanity of my own spiritual conceit what he was in for; and my heart went out to him because those last few steps are the hardest. What, then, is the magic formula of life that will shed light upon our quest for authenticity?

Try as I may, I could not explore the magic formula of life until I watched Lilou's interview with Dr. Wayne Dyer. I was *compelled* by an inner directive to find out if I was still projecting my own shadow, and I also wanted to see where Dyer was at in his own journey since the last time I flicked him off PBS; and as I watched the interview at his home in Maui, Hawaii it didn't take long to see that he no longer affected me the way he used to, because he no longer reflected that shadowy "it" factor that used to get under my skin.

There were two reasons for this: 1, he had resolved his "it" factor (the vanity of his spiritual conceit) with his leukemia and spiritual healing experience with John of God; and 2, I had also resolved my "it" factor with my spiritual healing with St. Padre Pio; and I was so touched by Lilou's interview with Dr. Wayne Dyer that I had to go for a long walk on the sandy beach of our beautiful Georgian Bay just to ground myself.

Dr. Wayne Dyer's leukemia and spiritual healing resolved his ego enough to open his heart up more to the *I Am* principle of life, and now the rest of his journey through life—his new mission, in fact—has taken on a passionate intensity to introduce the *I Am* principle of life to the world through writing and public talks; and by the *I Am* principle I mean the divine presence in each and every soul—that same *I Am* principle that God revealed to Moses: "And God said to Moses, 'I AM THAT I AM'", Exodus 3: 14; and centuries later Jesus revealed to the Jews, **"Verily, verily, I say unto you, before Abraham was, I am"** (John 8: 58)—the same *I Am* principle that I had also awakened to in my quest for my true self, which is why I no longer projected my "it" factor onto Dr. Wayne Dyer.

What a relief it was then to learn that I had resolved that aspect of my shadow personality responsible for my envy of writers like Zukav and Dyer, and as I walked the sandy beach yesterday I felt lighter but sad in a strange kind of way, because I had lost that precious part of myself that took secret pleasure in judging other people.

After St. Padre Pio slew the vanity of my spiritual conceit I wanted to throw up at what I used to be, and I saw that my healing experience with the Ascended Master boiled down to the simple realization that **our whole life can be reduced to a journey through vanity to humility**, just as Shelly captured in his archetypal poem *Ozymandias:*

> I met a traveler from an antique land
> Who said: Two vast and trunkless legs of stone
> Stand in the desert. Near them, on the sand,
> Half sunk, a shattered visage lies, whose frown,
> And wrinkled lip, and sneer of cold command,
> Tell that its sculptor well those passions read
> Which yet survive, stamped on these lifeless things,
> The hand that mocked them and the heart that fed;

> And on the pedestal these words appear:
> "My name is Ozymandias, king of kings:
> Look on my works, ye Mighty, and despair!"
> Nothing beside remains. Round the decay
> Of that colossal wreck, boundless and bare,
> The lone and level sands stretch far away.

I had been humbled by St. Padre Pio's redemptive love no less than the mighty King Ozymandias had been humbled by the leveling sands of time, and so had Dr. Wayne Dyer been humbled by his spiritual healing experience with John of God; and we were no longer burdened by the Ozymandian factor of our shadow personality—*blind conceit.*

Having said this, I can now explore the magic formula of life and delve into the mystery of *quantum spirituality post 2012…*

2. Quantum Spirituality Post 2012

St. Padre Pio was channeled by a very gifted intuitive empath for ten healing sessions that I had from August, 2010 to June 2011, and in one session he told me that the Mayan 2012 prophecy of a cosmic shift was going to be a smooth transition. "Nothing to worry about?" I asked, because of all the gloom and doom that attended the prophecy.

"No," he replied.

"It's just a smooth transition to a higher level of awareness?" I asked.

"Yes. He's even saying to a new way of thinking, a new way of being," said the woman who was channeling the Ascended Master.

"This is what he said about my writing. He said my writing is a new way of thinking, a new way of perceiving, a new way of understanding."

"Uh-hum. That's interesting. Okay, I didn't know this; but they are going to, they being those beings that we're not aware of on the other side, they're sending an infusion into the world. They're changing the vibration frequency of the world. It's already happened, but we're going to get the good benefit of it. The chaos we've been experiencing in the world has been a way of increasing the vibration of the planet, and in 2012 it's like a culmination, and there will be more, it's like an energy spreading around the world; there's more of a feeling, a higher vibration, a higher frequency coming in."

This "higher frequency" is what I'm inspired to call *quantum spirituality post 2012*— "a new way of thinking, a new way of being." But what does this mean? This is today's spiritual musing…

"Spirituality cannot be taught, but must be caught," said Paul Twitchell, the modern day founder of the ancient teachings of the Way of the Eternal; but spirituality has always been about energy, and the wisdom traditions of the world have always known how to tap into the energy of God—the energy of love that all spiritual healers speak of today.

Jesus knew how to tap into the energy of God. So much so that he realized his divine nature and became one with the energy of God. *"I and my Father are one,"* said Jesus; and he taught the world how to tap into the energy of God with his teaching.

Padre Pio, the humble Capuchin monk from Pietrelcina, Italy knew how to tap into the energy of God with *la via di sofforenza*. As he suffered for Christ (he suffered the stigmata for fifty years) he realized the energy of God, which he called his "glory." This "glory" is the same energy that Jesus implied when he talked about storing our "treasures" in heaven. Jesus called it "virtue." And I realized the energy of God as I "worked" on myself with Gurdjieff's teaching and the sayings of Jesus, to the point where I gave "birth" to my spiritual self one fine summer day in my mother's kitchen while she was kneading bread dough on the kitchen table.

Quantum spirituality post 2012 is about the energy of God, then. It is the sacred science of spiritual self-realization consciousness, which I was introduced to in my current lifetime through Gurdjieff's teaching of "work on oneself."

In a former life in ancient Greece I was taught the same sacred science by Pythagoras, and during the time of Jesus I studied the same hidden teaching with the Essenes at the Qumran community, and again in 15th Century Persia I was a member of a secret Sufi order that taught the same tradition; but not until my current lifetime did I manage to bring my karmic cycle to happy resolution. This is the purpose of *quantum spirituality post 2012*—to bring our personal karmic destiny into alignment with our pre-ordained spiritual destiny and complete our karmic cycle so we can continue evolution on a higher plane.

St. Padre Pio told me that karma is a choice, and that there are souls in the world today that live a karma-free life. I didn't understand what he meant by this, and he would not explain how to live a karma-free life despite how much I tried to get it out of him; but he did tell me that I would be doing research for another book and that I would come to an understanding of how soul can choose to live a karma-free life.

I started my research immediately after I finished writing *Healing with Padre Pio*, and my research took me to quantum physics, of which I knew less than nothing; but the more research I did on the Internet the more I saw how science and the ancient spiritual traditions of the world have found common ground in the unified field theory, or what Greg Braden has called the Divine Matrix, which is the ground of all being and Body of God.

Quantum spirituality post 2012 then is nothing more or less than the ancient science of spiritual self-realization consciousness in a modern scientific context; or, if you will, a holistic (albeit still "theoretical") understanding of man's multi-dimensional nature.

Science has always denied the spiritual nature of man, but not anymore. More and more scientists are bridging the wisdom of the ancient spiritual traditions of the world with quantum physics, and we are witnessing the birth of *quantum spirituality post 2012*.

Dr. Bruce Lipton's book *The Biology of Belief: Unleashing the Power of Consciousness, Matter and Miracles* is helping to bridge science with esoteric spirituality, and physicist Dr. Amit Goswami, who is pioneering the new paradigm of science called "science with consciousness," is also profoundly instrumental in birthing *quantum spirituality* with books like *The Self-Aware Universe*, *Physics of the Soul*, and *Quantum Creativity*, not to mention Braden's books *The Divine Matrix*, *The God Code*, and *The Spontaneous Healing of Belief*; and on and on. As St. Padre Pio said, "there's more of a higher vibration, a higher frequency coming in."

So the paradigm shift has begun, which according to the Ascended Master will culminate by December 21, 2012 and usher us into a golden age; and we can see this shift to unity consciousness with people like Gary Zukav, Dr. Wayne Dyer, Caroline Myss, Dr. Norman Shealy (the "Father of Holistic Medicine"), Deepak Chopra, and Amit Goswami to name only a few out of a growing network of spiritual teachers who are taking *quantum spirituality* out to the public with their own special connection with the energy of God.

Which is what I've done with *Healing with Padre Pio*, the story of my personal connection with the energy of God, and what I'm doing with this new volume of spiritual musings in which I hope to bring a little more clarity to the ancient science of spiritual self-realization consciousness that I've been inspired to call *quantum spirituality post 2012* to reflect today's scientific awakening to the energy of God but which the world has always known as the Way;

but, in all humility, I have no idea where my Muse is going to take me.

Hopefully, to new spiritual horizons…

3. The Miracle of the Individuation Process

I made a decision in my second year at university that changed my life. I had been cast adrift in a sea of endless speculation with my philosophy studies, and I was getting further and further away from my true self, which was ironic because I studied philosophy to find my true self; so I chose to stop depending upon the great minds of the world for answers and decided to build my life upon the truth of my own experiences instead.

"When the student is ready, the teacher appears," says the old saying; and my decision to become my own way to truth brought Gurdjieff into my life by way of P. D. Ouspensky's book *In Search of the Miraculous, Fragments of an Unknown Teaching*.

Gurdjieff's impossible teaching of "work on oneself" forced me to confront my shadow self and transform it with techniques like *self-remembering, non-identification, voluntary effort,* and *conscious suffering;* and the more I "worked" on myself, the more I awakened to the Word within, the omniscient guiding force of life.

The Word is the creative energy of God and reconciling power of Divine Spirit, or what Jesus called the "water of everlasting life" that flows through all life; and tapping into the "water of everlasting life" was what Jesus Christ's teaching was all about. This is why Gurdjieff called his teaching "esoteric Christianity."

Inevitably then, I incorporated Christ's teaching of eternal life into my path; and after years of "working" on myself with Gurdjieff's teaching and the sayings of Jesus I gave birth to my spiritual self, which I've written about in my novel *Keeper of the Flame*.

The Persian poet Farid ud-Din Attar wrote a Sufi teaching story of man's quest for God called *The Conference of the Birds*. Thousands of birds (souls) went on a quest for the Great Bird (God), and along the way they suffered many trials and tribulations. Out of all the birds that went on the quest for God, only thirty completed the journey; and when these fortunate few looked into the Face of God, guess what they saw? *Their own image!*

STUPIDITY IS NOT A GIFT OF GOD

The Conference of the Birds is an allegory that reveals the esoteric mysteries of the Sufi Path, but it was my reality; because when I tapped into the water of everlasting life I rode the turbulent currents of the Holy River of God all the way back to where all souls come from, and I too was blessed to look into the Face of God; but it took many years before I could put the truth of my experience into words.

I always had a strong desire to write a book on my own past lives ever since I read Jess Stearn's book *The Search for the Soul: Psychic Lives of Taylor Caldwell*, so I had seven past-life regressions when Penny and I relocated to Georgian Bay; but I did not expect to experience what I did in my fourth regression: *I went all the way back to the Body of God where all souls come from and experienced myself as an atom of God with Soul consciousness but no self-consciousness; and in the same regression I was sent into the lower worlds where I evolved through the life process of Planet Earth all the way up the ladder of evolution to my first primordial human lifetime where I experienced the actual dawning of my own reflective self-consciousness!*

When I was in the Body of God I *knew* that I did not have a reflective self-consciousness. I had Soul consciousness but no self-consciousness. In essence I was a Soul seed, and I was planted here (the Garden of Life, as the Sufis call this world) to evolve through the life process to acquire an individual identity, just as John Keats intuited in his inspired letter to his brother titled "The Vale of Soul Making."

Once I gave birth to my reflective self in my lifetime as a higher primate I created personal karma, because I had separated from the collective consciousness of my clan of ten or twelve members of which I was the alpha male, and I made personal choices instead of acting out of a collective will-to-be like the rest of my clan; and I brought my personal karma with me into future incarnations. And through the natural process of creating and resolving personal karma I grew in my own individual identity from one life to the next until I was ready to take evolution into my own hands, just as Gurdjieff said I would.

Gurdjieff believed that nature will only evolve us so far, and then we have to take evolution into our own hands to realize our full potential; and his teaching of "work on oneself" was all about taking evolution into our own hands, which was not easy to do.

Gurdjieff's teaching broke a lot of hearts. This is why Jesus said **"Many are called, but few are chosen."** But Paul Twitchell also said, *"If you don't get it right in this life, you will just keep coming back until you do,"* which heals the disillusioned soul.

Gurdjieff did not believe that everyone is born with an immortal soul. To make his point, he used the analogy of the oak tree which produces many acorn seeds but only a few will take root and grow into an oak tree; the rest go back to the recycling bin of nature and become fertilizer —or *"merde,"* as Gudjieff so crudely expressed it in French.

According to Gurdjieff, extreme life circumstances can constellate an immortal essence in some people; and this "embryonic soul" will reincarnate until nature can evolve it no further. And then one has to take evolution into his own hands to grow into the oak tree of his inherent potential — a promising but very, very hard teaching.

But Gurdjieff was fundamentally wrong in his perspective, because everyone is born with a spark of divine consciousness. As St. Padre Pio told me in one of my spiritual healing sessions, we are all part of the Whole; so how can we not be an immortal part of God? *Which is what precisely quantum physics is coming to realize!*

My regression to the Body of God confirmed this, and my evolution through life also confirmed that nature will evolve the atom of God until it gives birth to its own reflective self-consciousness, which is our human self; and when we finally realize that nature can do no more to satisfy our longing for wholeness we have to take evolution into our own hands to fulfill our encoded pre-ordained spiritual destiny and realize our divine nature.

This is what Gary Zukav intuited when he told Lilou Mace that we have to bring our personality into alignment with our soul. He took evolution into his own hands and connected with the energy of God and caught a glimpse of the magic formula of life, which is to reconcile our karmic destiny with our spiritual destiny and make them into one path that St. Padre Pio called the path of the selfless self, which essentially is the path of love.

Our karmic destiny is born of the choices we make in life, which becomes our personal path; and our encoded spiritual destiny is to become God-realized souls. A God-realized soul has evolved in spiritual consciousness enough to realize that it is one with the *I Am* principle of life, which Dr. Wayne Dyer realized when he connected with the energy of God through his personal path and I realized with my own eclectic path.

The central mystery of life then is man's *a priori* need for total self-identity, which is God-realization consciousness. We're all born to grow in our own identity, and the only way we can do that is to bring our karmic destiny into agreement with our spiritual destiny; this is why the Sufis say that there are as many ways to God as there are souls of man, and why St. Padre Pio told me that life is a journey of the self. This is why our greatest need in life is to become who we are meant to be—*our divine self.*

The real mystery is connecting with the energy of God. This is what religion and spiritual paths are supposed to help us do. But one does not have to belong to a religion or take up a spiritual path to connect with the energy of God, because the natural process of karmic reconciliation will do that for us—like the poet who *has* to write poetry, the musician who *has* to play music, or the artist who *has* to paint; they all tap into the creative life force with their personal path and grow in who they are meant to be.

Our karmic destiny will eventually compel us to connect with the energy of God, if not in this lifetime the next. This happens when one is called to live his karmic destiny, whatever one's karmic destiny may be—art, poetry, medicine, or whatever; and as one lives his calling he satisfies his longing to be whole and nourishes his inherent need for God-realization consciousness, which is why St. Padre Pio told me that there is more than one way in life. This was his way of telling me that our own life is the way to our true self.

When I left university to find my own way in life little did I know that I was stepping onto the age-old path to total self-realization consciousness, because to find my true self I had to go through my unresolved karmic self just as Jesus said I would: **"He that findeth his life shall lose it; and he that loseth his life for my sake shall find it"** (Math. 10: 39).

Like the thirty birds in the Sufi allegory, I had to "die" to my karmic self to see my divine self in the Face of God. In effect then, we have to bring ego into agreement with our spiritual self (align our personality with our soul, as Gary Zukav expressed it), and the only way to do that is to connect with the energy of God; because the more we connect with the energy of God, the more we transcend ourselves until one fine day we can say *I Am that I Am* because we are God-realized Souls.

As I came to realize, the self is the mystery of life. The reflective self that I gave birth to in my first primordial human lifetime was the birth of a new "I" of God, which is the alpha and omega of life. This is why Paul Twitchell said, "God needs man as much as man needs God," because as we individuate the un-self-realized consciousness of life we grow in our divine nature and expand the consciousness of God. This is the real meaning of *I Am that I Am*, and the miracle of the individuation process—*God becoming God!*

4. Deus Ex Machina

Is humanity in need of *deus ex machina* (divine redeemer)? I believe it is, and according to Ascended Master St. Padre Pio (among other sources: past-life regressionist Dolores Cannon, psychic Diana Cooper, and intuitive Penney Peirce), *deux ex machina* has already begun to save humanity from its karmically scripted plotline of self-destruction.

"They're changing the vibration frequency of the world," said St. Padre Pio in one of my spiritual healing sessions, in reference to "those" on the other side that are infusing the world with spiritual energy to raise the vibration frequency of world consciousness to engender what he called "a new way of thinking, a new way of being."

"Those" on the other side are the redeeming *deus ex machina* who have put aside the cosmic law of non-interference to help the world, because it's quite obvious that we can't help ourselves; our ecosystem is collapsing, and time, according to Dr. David Suzuki, the environmental activist and host of *The Nature of Things*, is quickly running out.

Deus ex machina may save the day for us (hopefully it will), but the ball will always be in our court because we fate ourselves to repeat our selfish patterns of behavior. Only we can reconcile our karmic destiny with our spiritual destiny to realize our essential purpose in life, and saving the world only buys us more time to come to this realization; hence the irony of our situation, because the purpose of raising the world's consciousness is to wake us up to our karmic responsibility. The Greek poet Cleanthes understood our dilemma long ago, and he wrote a poem that captures our predicament:

> Lead me, o Zeus
> And thou o destiny,
> The way I am bid by thee to go;
> To follow I am willing,

For were I recusant
I do but make myself a slave,
And still must follow.

We are all slaves to our own karma, which has finally brought the world to the brink of ecological disaster; that's why we need *deus ex machina*. We've had many opportunities to "flush our toilet," but we let the refuse of our karma build up to the point where it has plugged up the whole system of natural evolution, and we need help. Just as Hercules diverted the water of two mighty rivers to flush clean the Augean stables, so too do we need a flood of spiritual consciousness to flush clean the karmic toxins of our world.

Gurdjieff knew that we needed help as far back as 1911. He offered a keen analysis of the emerging modern dilemma. "There's a growth of personality at the expense of essence, a growth of the artificial, the unreal, and what is foreign, at the cost of the natural, the real, and what is one's own," he said, which he called "the terror of the situation."

To avoid complete disaster it was necessary to achieve world harmony as soon as possible; but according to Gurdjieff it could not be achieved by politics, philosophy, religion, or any organized movement that treated man in the mass. It could only be accomplished through the individual development of man, which was why he introduced his dam-busting teaching of radical self-transformation to the western world.

Gurdjieff maintained that if enough individuals could develop themselves even partially into genuine natural beings, each such individual would then be able to convince and win over as many as a hundred others, who would, each in his turn, be able to influence another hundred and so on; but here we are one century later in 2012 on the brink of disaster, and despite all the Gurdjieff study groups in the world we need *deus ex machina*.

In the Forward to the 2010 Edition of *The Undiscovered Self* that C. G. Jung wrote in 1956, Jungian scholar Sonu Shamdasani wrote: "He (Jung) argued that the only solution to the seemingly catastrophic developments in the world lay in the individual turning within and resolving the individual aspects of his collective conflicts," which Jung, the wounded healer, did himself and devoted the rest of his life to helping the world to do.

But that was a tall order half a century ago, and it's a much taller order today because the insatiable archetypal patterns of man's egoic nature have made it virtually impossible to shift the karmic paradigm from serving oneself to serving life, which is the only way we can break the back of our collective karmic beast; that's why we need *deus ex machina*. How, then, will this infusion of spiritual energy help us?

I'm going to step out on a limb here, because this is not my field of expertise; or is it? After all, the Way is the solution to our dilemma, personally and collectively; and if there is anything that I am certain of in life, it is my gnosis of the Way.

I came into this life to find the Way, and despite my circumstances I became a seeker at a very early age; and in my twenties I found Gurdjieff, whose teaching awakened me to the Word. This attracted me to Christ's teaching, because Jesus was the Word made manifest. ***"I am the way, the truth, and the life,"*** said Jesus; ***"whosoever drinketh of the water that I shall give him shall never thirst; but the water that I shall give him shall be in him a well of water springing up into everlasting life"*** (John 14: 6, and 4: 14).

I incorporated Christ's teaching into my path and brought my karmic destiny into alignment with my spiritual destiny and shifted my center of gravity from my lower to higher self one summer day in my mother's kitchen, so I can speak about the Way with the certainty of one who has lived the Way consciously and given birth to his spiritual self.

To live the Way consciously we have to take karmic responsibility for our own life, which means that we have to be aware of the consequences of our actions. If we pollute the air and land and lakes and rivers and oceans with toxic chemicals, we're going to suffer the consequences of our collective actions; which we're experiencing today with global warming, dead zones in the oceans, and contamination of our major food sources.

The karmic consequences of our actions are so obvious today that we have been shocked into awareness, and still we continue to pollute our beautiful planet. Are we that stupid? Why can't we stop? Why do we continue on this path of self-destruction?

Can the alcoholic stop drinking without help? Carl Jung, the eminent psychologist and founder of analytical psychology didn't think so; and, as irony would have it, he was instrumental in the foundation of Alcoholics Anonymous by curing Rowland H. who shared his story with Bill Wilson who founded Alcoholics Anonymous. Jung told Rowland H. that if he wanted to stop drinking he had to appeal to a higher power, which he did; and to heal the world of its compulsive addiction to karmic patterns of self-destruction we also have to appeal to a higher power—hence, *deus ex machina*.

We need all the help we can get to cure the world of our addiction to self-destructive patterns of behavior because we can't do it on our own. We have tried, but we cannot do it without help from a higher power; so those beings from the other side are assisting us today by infusing the planet with spiritual energy to raise the world's consciousness, which accounts for the explosion of interest in Angels, spiritual healings, past-life regression therapy, and all kinds of phenomena of a spiritual nature as witnessed in the movies and YouTube and unending stream of books on the emerging new spiritual consciousness.

With the help of *deus ex machina* old thought patterns are breaking up and new thought patterns are created, because the law of entrainment (which states that two resonances existing in the same place must combine and adjust to a single resonance) is forcing the world to synchronize with a higher level of consciousness.

That's what St. Padre Pio meant when he said that the world is going to experience "a new way of thinking, a new way of being," which boils down to shifting our paradigm from self-serving patterns of self-destruction to life-serving patterns of holistic healing and harmonious living. As Cleanthes implied in his poem, we can walk alongside our destiny or be dragged by it. It seems that the world refuses to walk alongside its destiny, and it is being assisted by a higher power that has come to our aid.

It's hard to imagine, but the soul of the world has grown too big for the self-serving ego of the world, and something has to give—hence catastrophes like Hurricane Katrina, the Haitian earthquake disaster, Japan's devastating tsunami, Hurricane Sandy, draughts and crop failures, and economic/political meltdowns that are necessary to break up old self-serving karmic patterns of behavior, and I for one welcome *deus ex machina*.

5. The Riddle of Atheism

Inspired by an article in Psychology Today Magazine
June 2012
"The Atheist at the Breakfast Table"

I believed in God, but I loved the atheist philosophies of Jean Paul Sartre and Albert Camus when I was studying philosophy at university. I especially loved Camus' book of essays *The Myth of Sisyphus*; but I had to say goodbye to these writers because they had served their purpose of introducing me to the *being* and *non-being* nature of man.

"I am what I am not, and I am not what I am," concluded Sartre with his philosophy of *being* and *nothingness*, and Camus brought his philosophy of the absurd to its logical conclusion by imagining Sisyphus happy forever rolling his rock up a hill in Hades; but I *knew* deep inside that my life was not "a useless passion," nor could I ever imagine Sisyphus happy condemned to his senseless fate for offending the gods; so I thanked the philosophers for their insights into the nature of man's contingent physical existence, and with Gurdjieff's teaching under my arm I left university to forge my own path in life.

I found the Way as I "worked" on myself with Gurdjieff's teaching, and I liberated myself from the paradigm of creative opposites—the *being* and *non-being* aspects of my nature and driving force of the natural individuation process of life; but I never stopped thinking about Sartre and Camus whose courageous efforts to make sense of life fueled my passion to find my true self, and I had to find out why they did not believe in God. I simply had to know, because it bothered me that these two great philosophers (both Nobel Laureates)—not to mention the formidable mind of Bertrand Russell whose seductive book of essays *Why I Am Not A Christian* gave countless people the courage to call themselves atheists—could not part the veil of the mind and see the spiritual dimension of life.

STUPIDITY IS NOT A GIFT OF GOD

The "gadfly" of Athens however parted the veil and saw that our imperishable divine essence was trapped in the *being* and *non-being* individuation process of our perishable mortal human life. "There is a doctrine uttered in secret that man is a prisoner who has no right to open the door of his prison and run away," said the Socrates in Plato's *Phaedo*, and he found a way out of the existential prison of *being* and *becoming* which he symbolically revealed in his famous allegory of the cave in Plato's *Republic*.

For Socrates the way out of our prison of *being* and *becoming* was by way of virtue, of which goodness was the highest and most liberating; and like all teachers of the Way he realized that to escape from our prison (the recurring cycle of life and death) we have to transform the consciousness of our human self—which Jesus referred to in his teaching of spiritual liberation as "losing" one's life to "save" one's life.

"He that loveth his life shall lose it; and he that hateth his life in this world shall keep it unto life eternal," said Jesus (John 12:25); which means that one has to "die" to his lower self, or in Gurdjieffian terms *transform* the consciousness of his human self to realize his divine essence, which Socrates also addressed with his philosophy.

"I deem that the true disciple of philosophy is likely to be misunderstood by other men; they do not perceive that he is forever pursuing death and dying," he said in the *Phaedo*; and by "death" he meant liberation of our divine essence from the consciousness of our human self, which we can do with the purifying power of the noble virtues, especially goodness; this is why I concluded that the ultimate purpose of life is to simply be a good person. "And what is purification but the separation of soul from the body," said Socrates; "as I was saying before, the habit of soul gathering and collecting herself into herself, out of all the courses of the body, the dwelling in her own place alone, as in another life, so also in this, as far as she can; the release of soul from the chains of the body."

Whether it's Gurdjieff's teaching of self-transformation, Christ's teaching of eternal life, or Socrates' liberating philosophy of virtue, it is the same omniscient guiding force of life known throughout history as the Way (Aldous Huxley, author of *Brave New World* called it the "perennial philosophy" and wrote a book by that title); but whatever teaching one embraces, unless we *live* it we will never resolve the paradoxical nature of our *being* and *non-being* and realize our divine nature. This is why Sartre and Camus got stuck in the existential dimension of life and could not find the key to their prison door.

The key to our prison door is the reconciling energy of the Way. Socrates speaks to the reconciling energy of the Way when he talks about *"soul gathering and collecting herself into herself out of all the courses of the body"* by living the inherently self-transcending values of the virtuous life. Soul is trapped in the consciousness of our ego self, and by living a life of virtue one purifies ego and realizes his spiritual self.

Gurdjieff's and Christ's teachings also purify ego, but it doesn't really matter what teachings of the Way one lives because the Way is Divine Spirit, which is the life force; so the inherently self-reconciling power of the Way exists in all dimensions of life—be one a writer, a doctor, physicist, or whatever; and we are forever transforming our consciousness through the natural individuation process of life. But life will only take us so far, and then we have to take evolution into our own hands to realize our divinely encoded potential.

If you will then, Socrates, Jesus, and Gurdjieff merely concentrated the reconciling power of Divine Spirit into their own teaching of the Way—as Caroline Myss, Gary Zukav, Dr. Wayne Dyer, Deepak Chopra, Amit Goswami and every person who has connected with the energy of God does as they live their own path; and by incorporating the wisdom of the Way into my path I transformed my consciousness and realized my true self. That's how I solved the riddle of atheism that Sartre and Camus had saddled me with.

I was so intimidated by their writing that I dreaded reading them; but once I realized that our mind was the biggest obstacle to realizing our divine nature I stopped being intimidated by their brilliance, because as I lived the Way I resolved the paradoxical nature of my *being* and *non-being* and transcended myself.

That's when I brought Sartre's philosophy to its proper conclusion. **"I am what I am not, and I am not what I am,"** I said along with Sartre, because I was acutely conscious of the same life-fatiguing existential process of *being* and *becoming* (Sartre's "useless passion" and Camus' absurd Sisyphean fate); but because I had learned how to gather and collect myself into myself (reconcile my lower self with my higher self), I was able to add to Sartre's incomplete philosophy, **"I am both, but neither: I am Soul,"** because I had given birth to my spiritual self in my mother's kitchen one day and transcended myself; and from the perspective of the Soul Plane of Consciousness I could finally see why they did not believe in God—*because they were blinded to their spiritual nature by their own mind!*

As brilliant as Sartre and Camus were, they had trapped themselves in the existential consciousness of *being* and *becoming*, the never-ending cycle of life and death; and not until the natural process of evolution makes the atheist ready for the Way will they find the key to the prison door of their mind and escape. As H. P. Blavatsky said in *The Voice of the Silence*, "The Mind is the great Slayer of the Real; let the disciple slay the Slayer."

"Many are called but few are chosen," Jesus tells us; but mercifully it doesn't matter if we find the key in this lifetime or not, because we will just keep coming back until we do because we are all pre-destined to realize our divine nature.

6. Healing the Soul of the World One Soul at a Time

For a spiritual healing to occur the mind has to be in agreement with Divine Spirit; or as St. Padre Pio put it, "you have to be in a place of understanding for a spiritual healing," and my novel *Healing with Padre Pio* is all about how he brought me to that place of understanding for my spiritual healing to occur.

I may be speaking out of turn, but I have the distinct feeling that my spiritual healing is in keeping with the spiritual help that the world is getting from *deus ex machina*—like the alcoholic who goes to Alcoholics Anonymous for help when he hits bottom and comes to the understanding that he needs help from a higher power to heal his addiction.

The world has hit bottom with global warming, crop failures, depletion of fish stocks, calamitous hurricanes, political meltdowns and social unrest, and like the alcoholic who does not want to admit that he has a drinking problem the world is finally beginning to realize that we have a problem and need help; and like the alcoholic who turns to a higher power for help, so is the world turning to a higher power—hence the increasing number of people today that are channeling this higher power.

I needed help from a higher power to heal my wounded Christian soul; that's why I went to a spiritual healer who channeled Ascended Master Saint Padre Pio. I had some very deep anger issues with my Roman Catholic faith which I brought with me from my past lifetime in Paris, France in the 17th Century; but in order for my spiritual healing to occur I had to be brought to a place of understanding first.

Like the alcoholic in denial of his addiction, I was in denial of my spiritual hubris; and unless I acknowledged my blind conceit I would never be in a place of understanding for a spiritual healing to occur, and St. Padre Pio was the ideal person to bring me to that place of understanding because his humility was so devastating it slew the vanity of my spiritual conceit and the redemptive love of God could finally heal my wounded soul.

STUPIDITY IS NOT A GIFT OF GOD

In like manner, the world has been in denial of its scientific hubris for so long that it failed to acknowledge the harm it has been doing to the planet; but like the alcoholic that hits bottom the world can no longer deny the karmic consequences of its actions and is in desperate need of help from a higher power, hence the proliferation of spiritual healers and teachers that are being introduced to the world through the phenomenon of the Internet.

Until I started watching Lilou Mace interview all these spiritual healers and teachers throughout the world on her *Juicy Living Tour,* I had no idea how much the omniscient guiding force of Divine Spirit was doing to heal the wounded soul of the world; and the more I watched her interview these remarkable people, the more I came to the realization that the world is now in a place of understanding to resolve the karma responsible for bringing the world to the brink of destruction—which explains all the spiritual healings that people are experiencing throughout the world.

For example, a humble man called John of God from a small community in Brazil has healed thousands of people as an agent of God; not to mention the countless number of souls that are waking up to Divine Spirit's guidance through motivational speakers and writers like Caroline Myss, Dr. Wayne Dyer, Andrew Harvey (the founder of *Sacred Activism*), and quantum activist Amit Goswami to name only a select few.

Now that quantum physics has posited the unified field theory that proves we are not separate from the whole and affect the whole with the choices we make, science has become aware of its hubris and has been brought to a place of understanding where the wounded soul of the world can be healed; and although some people expected a dramatic shift to a higher state of consciousness with the Mayan December 21, 2012 prophecy, healing the soul of the world happens slowly and almost imperceptibly one soul at a time—a slow, smooth transition from the selfish-negative to the unselfish-positive, just as Padre Pio said it would be. Indeed, 2013 augurs well for the world…

7. The Co-existence of Parallel Worlds

St. Padre Pio gave me a riddle to solve. In my tenth and final spiritual healing session he told me that I have lived my same life over again three times, and my current life is one of those times. He told me that I chose to be reborn into my same life as Orest Stocco to achieve a different outcome because I wasn't content with my first outcome.

This explained the strange dream I had a number of years ago. I was an elderly man walking up to the post office in my hometown, which in itself isn't peculiar; but what made this dream so memorable was how I felt as I was walking to the post office: I was not happy with my life. I felt incomplete, like I had failed to do what I was born to do.

That's why St. Padre Pio's comment about me coming back to live my same life over again made sense to me, because this time around I have completed what I was born to do—*which was to find a way out of the recurring cycle of life and death.*

St. Padre Pio's exact words were: "In your first outcome, you would continue to be close-minded about that other religion (my current spiritual path, the Way of the Eternal), and in that past lifetime you were; and now here you are to understand that you can be more open about what everybody experiences."

I was close-minded the first time I lived my life, but now I am more open to other people's experiences; but this whole concept of being reborn into one's same life again to achieve a different outcome came as a complete surprise to me.

When I discovered Dr. Bruce Goldberg's book *Past Lives, Future Lives Revealed* I was shocked to learn that one could be taken to a future lifetime under hypnosis, but coincidentally enough it confirmed a strange dream that I had of being born into a future life as a very precocious young writer; but the idea of being reborn into my same life to achieve a different outcome jolted me out of my paradigm and inspired *The Summoning of Noman, The True Story of My Parallel Life.*

I had to find out what it meant to be reborn into my same life, so I began to do some research. I honestly didn't know where to start, so I began with a deeper study of dreams and C. G. Jung, and I also started a new dream journal.

As I researched the dreaming process online, one window opened onto another until I came upon quantum physics and multidimensional universes; and I may have found the answer to the mind-boggling riddle of parallel lives.

It came to me yesterday as I was listening to Dolores Cannon on You Tube. She was talking about the Mayan 2012 prophecy and the new Earth, and something she said about what happens to people when the Earth splits in two and the new Earth goes to the fifth dimension clicked for me. She didn't quite understand how this ascension of people to a higher dimension worked exactly, but she made a comment about people dropping out of our lives when one ascends with the new Earth, and in a flash I got a fleeting insight of Soul's coexistence in a multidimensional universe; or, as it is called today, "multiverse."

I discovered Dolores Cannon four or five years ago when I was doing research on the mystic Essenes for a book I was writing. She wrote a book called *Jesus and the Essenes*, which confirmed what I have always felt about the Essenes because I had a past lifetime as an Essene during the time of Jesus. My name was Samuel, and I was a scribe at Qumran.

Dolores Cannon is a past-life regressionist, and through her clients she has learned some incredible things about Soul's purpose in life and the evolution of the planet, which she has written about in a series of books; but to appreciate the riddle of living one's same life over again to achieve a different outcome I have to give some context for my life.

At the risk of saying something that I cannot verify but which I believe to be true, I've always had a vague memory of making a bet with a group of fellow souls on the other side that I could come back into my next incarnation and find my way out of the recurring cycle of life and death on my own without anyone's help, as such.

Since I've already written about my spiritual quest elsewhere, suffice to say that I became a seeker at an early age. I found Gurdjieff in university through P. D. Ouspensky's book *In Search of the Miraculous,* and with his teaching I awakened to the Way and transformed the consciousness of my lower self enough to shift my center of gravity from my lower to higher self. In Christ's words, I "died" to my life to "find" my life. In effect, I gave birth to my spiritual self and broke my recurring karmic cycle of life and death.

I had this experience in my mother's kitchen one day while she was kneading bread dough on the kitchen table, and from the moment that I experienced my own immortality I have never doubted that I am an eternal soul; so I accomplished what I came here to do. That's why I said to Penny the other day, "I can die anytime now. I'm ready."

Of course I'd love to grow old along with her, because in the words of Robert Browning, "the best is yet to be." The point is that I'm no longer driven to find the key, because I have opened the door of life's prison and stepped into that higher dimension that Dolores Cannon was talking about with the splitting of the new Earth.

An hour or so after listening to Dolores Cannon I was nudged to research David Icke's book *Remember Who You Are* on Amazon. I read the free sample of the Kindle version of his book, and by "coincidence" I learned something that confirmed my insight into the co-existence of multi-dimensional universes. David Icke wrote: *"Creation is an infinite range of interpenetrating frequency 'worlds,' and the frequency range that we decode becomes our sense of reality. But all the other 'worlds' share the same 'space', just like radio stations and analogue television channels."*

That's a scientific explanation for the co-existence of parallel worlds, but the only way I can make sense of this is to posit that Soul exists in the Eternal Now because time does not exist as such. Soul is who we are. Soul is our eternal spiritual self, and our personalities are the identities that we create with each new life that we live, and our personality-identities exist in the space-time dimension; and only when we focus, or "tune" into a particular time-space dimension (like tuning into a radio station) do we become aware of a particular lifetime—like my current lifetime.

The life that I'm currently living is the life that I have "tuned" into. But I have lived this life before, which means that I am now living my same life in a separate time-space reality. In other words, I am living my two same lives simultaneously in parallel worlds.

This is why I started a new dream journal. Dreams are messages from Soul, and I feel that my dreams will tell me about both of my lives as Orest Stocco; and, hopefully, I will learn what my **choice point of entry** was to my current lifetime, and by this I mean the experience that shifted my focus from my first life as Orest Stocco to my current life.

But I suspect I know what that experience was—a daimonically driven poem that I wrote in grade twelve called "Noman," which was set free from the depths of my unconscious by the morality play "Everyman" that played upon my conscience from the day I read it several days before writing "Noman," and which became the inspiration for my new book *The Summoning of Noman, The True Story of My Parallel Life*.

So I may have the answer to the riddle of my parallel life; but I'm still trying to wrap my head around the interpenetrating realities of frequency worlds. I suspect that we come in and out of our parallel lives without realizing it, forever influencing our past and future lives with the choices we make in our current life; but that's another musing.

8. My Journey to Authenticity

We are not one, but two; and learning how to make the two into one is what the journey to authenticity is all about, because only when we are centered in the consciousness of one harmoniously integrated self can we be wholly authentic. This was my journey, which did not begin in earnest until I heard a voice in my mind one desperately lonely night ask me the question, *"why do you lie?"*

I had come to a dead end with Gurdjieff's teaching and had no idea where to turn next to continue my quest for my true self; that's when I heard a voice ask in my mind the question that fueled my quest with so much energy that I finally broke the karmic grip my shadow self had upon me and I took Gurdjieff's teaching to a whole new level.

It's not surprising that Gurdjieff's transformative teaching would eventually lead me to C. G. Jung's psychology of the self and the individuation process, because Gurdjieff's concept of the false personality was the same as Jung's concept of the shadow self; both addressed the repressed unconscious aspect of our conscious personality, and until they were harmoniously integrated one would never be authentically himself.

This was my task. To find my true self I had to authenticate my false personality; but how could I do that if I did not believe I was false? I learned years later from Jung that it takes great moral courage to see one's own shadow, and that's what the voice in my mind wanted me to do with the startling question *"why do you lie?"*

I did not know whose voice it was, or why it asked me that question because I did not believe myself to be a liar. I was a truth seeker. But the very nature of how the question was asked (in my own mind!) made me stop and pay attention to my life; and pay attention I did. From the moment I heard that voice I began to turn my attention inward in a way that Gurdjieff's technique of *self-remembering* never let me do; and the more attention I paid to my life—my thoughts, feelings, and actions—the more I began to discern my false personality; and that's when I took Gurdjieff's teaching to a whole new level.

Gurdieff said something in Ouspensky's book *In Search of the Miraculous* that put the question *"why do you lie?"* squarely into my lap: "To speak the truth is the most difficult thing in the world, and one must study a great deal and for a long time to be able to speak the truth. The wish alone is not enough. **To speak the truth one must know what the truth is and what a lie is, and first of all in oneself.** And this nobody wants to know."

I did not want to see myself as a liar. Who does? But the more attention I paid to myself, the more conscious I became of myself; and I began to see that lying has so many various and subtle shades of self-deception that it takes an acute sense of moral awareness to see them; so that simple question *"why do you lie?"* forced me to raise the bar of my moral values. And that's when I began to "see" my own shadow!

My shadow was my false personality, but it was not in my conscious field of awareness. So well integrated was my shadow with my conscious personality that I had no idea whatsoever that I was more false than real—or, to use the Sartrean language of existential psychology, I was more inauthentic than authentic, and I lived my life in what Sartre called *mauvaise foi* (bad faith). And I spent years shifting my center of gravity from my false to real self, which I could not have done without Gurdjieff's teaching and the sayings of Jesus that opened up their secrets of self-transformation to me.

I have already written about my experience as a waiter in the Nipigon Inn Hotel in my hometown in *Old Whore Life, Exploring the Shadow Side of Karma* when I *non-identified* with my work and the strippers on stage (another Gurdjieffian technique for "work on oneself") with such focused attention that I literally felt a "snap" inside me; and the moment I felt that "snap" I was liberated from the fixed grip that my unconscious shadow had upon my personality, so I need not relate that experience here. Suffice to say that I actually experienced the miraculous shift in my center of gravity from my false self to my real self; or, to be philosophically specific, I shifted my center of gravity from my *non-being* to my *being* state of consciousness—*from my inauthentic to authentic self!*

From the moment I made this dramatic ontological shift in self-consciousness I no longer had an unconscious impulse to falseness, which was something that I never understood and was unable to make sense of until I made a study of Jung's psychology of the self; and from that night on I was free of the unconscious hold that my shadow had upon me, and I could instantly tell a lie from the truth in my own mind the moment it appeared.

This was an amazing intuitive gift; but I would not wish the price that I had to pay for this gift upon anyone. And yet this is the price that one must pay if one is centered in their false self and wants to be authentic. Not everyone is centered in their false self, of course; it depends upon how much power one's shadow has over their conscious personality.

My shadow had so much karmic power from my past lives that once it became fused with my family shadow (my family's false personality) my shadow melded with my conscious personality (I can't be specific, but I think I was in grade ten when this happened) and I began to have the most uneasy feeling that I was false in everything that I said and did, as if everything I said and did was colored in bad faith; and not until I "worked" on myself with Gurdjieffian discipline (which I brought to a feverish intensity that night in the hotel as I waited on tables) did I break the hold that my archetypal false self had upon me.

From that night on I never again had that shadow impulse to falseness, because I had shifted my center of gravity from the *non-being* to the *being* aspect of my nature—or, if you will, from my inauthentic to authentic self; and one cannot imagine the relief that I experienced when I felt that inner "snap" as I served tables and *non-identified* with the seductive strippers from Montreal as they gyrated their naked bodies on stage!

It took years of "working" on myself, but I finally answered the question *"why do you lie?"* I lied because I was in the grips of my shadow self; and not until I shifted my center of gravity from my inauthentic to authentic self did I stop lying unconsciously; and to this day it takes an enormous effort of will for me to tell a conscious lie. But my quest for my true self did not stop there; I still had a long way to go.

9. Chance or Divine Intervention?

"Even the road to nowhere leads somewhere."
Robert H. Hopcke

    I was rereading *Jung the Mystic* by Gary Lachman on our front deck yesterday, and because of Jung's fascination with *Thus Spoke Zarathustra* I dug up Nietzsche's book and was reading that also; but as I was reading I remembered that I had read a book years ago on Nietzsche by Rudolph Steiner (*Friedrich Nietzsche: A Fighter for Freedom*), so I went to the basement to look for it, and as I was digging through my books I came upon Robert H. Hopcke's book *There Are No Accidents, Synchronicities and the Stories of Our Lives* and I got the strongest nudge to read it again for reasons I wasn't aware of but which became apparent to me the moment I went back out to the deck to resume reading.

    I've experienced some extraordinary coincidences in my life, one in particular which confirmed my belief that coincidences (specifically synchronicities, a term coined by C. G. Jung to mean meaningful coincidences) are God's way of guiding souls through life, and as I read Hopcke's book on synchronicities and the stories of our lives I was certain that this was the entry point I needed to write a musing on the Way that has been crying to be written ever since I began writing my first volume of spiritual musings (*Just Going with the Flow, And Other Spiritual Musings*), because synchronicities gave me the context I needed to explain the elusive mystery of how the Way works in life.

    The Way is the omniscient guiding force of life. It is the Voice of God calling souls back home to the Higher Worlds where we came from, and it speaks to us through signs, symbols, chance occurrences, coincidences, synchronicities, dreams, waking dreams, "book angels" and any way possible to get our attention—especially and unequivocally so through Jesus who said, **"I am the way, the truth, and the life; no man cometh unto the Father but by me."** But for what purpose? What does God want us to hear? This is what I have been strongly nudged to explore in today's spiritual musing…

There are multiple points of entry to explore this haunting question, but I'm inclined to go with an incredible dream I had with C. G. Jung five years ago, several weeks after the startling waking dream experience I had that inspired my novel *The Waking Dream* in which the eminent psychologist C. G. Jung plays a central role.

A waking dream is a dream experience that manifests in our life when we are awake. It stands apart from other experiences because it is fraught with so much symbolic meaning, and mine was so charged with symbolic meaning that I had to write a whole book to unpack it; hence my novel memoir *The Waking Dream*.

Briefly, one Sunday morning five years ago I went out to give an estimate for a painting job in Midhurst just north of Barrie, and I brought my mini tape recorder with me because I was working on my third "Soul talk" book, *The Soul of Happiness*; and as I drove to Midland first to pick up my Sunday paper and then on to Midhurst to give my painting estimate, I talked my final chapter "The Ontology of Happiness" into my recorder that I had hanging off my rearview mirror.

My first "Soul talk" book was *The Way of Soul*, the book that C. G. Jung read on the other side but which was not even transcribed yet let alone published. Time is different on the other side however, and Jung had read my book and wanted to discuss it with me; so he came to me in a dream. It was ironic that the world's onetime foremost interpreter of dreams should contact me by way of a dream, and the irony did not escape us; and after we had our little laugh he got right to the point. He told me that he had crossed over to the other side without having solved the central mystery of his life, which he defined as "the alpha and omega of the self," and he was anxious to talk to me about my book *The Way of Soul*.

My "Soul talk" books were born of a technique I had cultivated not unlike Jung's "active imagination" technique in which one abandons to the creative unconscious— something like automatic writing, but not quite; and by the time I got to my third book *The Soul of Happiness* I could tap into the creative unconscious so effectively that when I got home from Midhurst I had completed my chapter "The Ontology of Happiness" and was so magnetized by the creative energy from my "Soul talk" that when I rested my feet on our coffee table in the living room after a late breakfast to relax and read the paper the energy poured out of my energy field into the brass rim of our round glass coffee table until it was charged enough to magnetize and charge the brass eagle sitting in the center of the coffee table, and right before our eyes (thank God Penny was there to witness it), the thick smoked glass of our coffee table imploded and shattered into half a dozen pieces!

"Oh Orest, what have you done now?" Penny said to me, completely nonplussed.

It took a few minutes for us to settle down, but when it dawned on me what had just happened I exclaimed, *"That's a waking dream!"*

Shattering the smoked glass ("glass darkly") of our coffee table was a waking dream that symbolically pointed to the fact that I had shattered a hole through the "glass darkly" of the Mental Plane of Consciousness with the powerful vibrations of the last chapter of my third "Soul talk" book ("The Ontology of Happiness," which was about transforming the consciousness of our ego self that obfuscates our perception of our spiritual self on the Soul Plane of Consciousness), and several weeks later Carl Jung came to me in a dream to talk about "the alpha and omega of the self," and I made our conversation central to my novel *The Waking Dream.* In the simplest terms possible, shattering the smoked glass of our coffee table was symbolic of shattering the difficult-to-see through consciousness of our ego (mental) self that keeps us trapped on the Mental Plane of Consciousness.

And people wonder where novels come from. Now I can explain how the Way guides us back home to God, and the part that synchronicity plays in our life…

I would not have solved the mystery of the alpha and omega of the self had I not experienced what I did during one of my seven past-life regressions. In my fourth regression I was brought back to the Body of God where all souls come from, and I experienced myself as an atom of God with Soul consciousness but no self-consciousness; and I was then sent into the lower worlds to grow and evolve through life to acquire self-identity.

The miraculous dawning of my reflective self-consciousness occurred in my lifetime as a higher primate, which I experienced in my regression. I was the alpha male of a clan of ten or twelve higher primates, and from the moment that I gave birth to my reflective self (it was a dim sense of self-awareness, but enough to set me apart from my clan) I began to create personal karma; and with personal karma I created an individual karmic destiny that played itself out from lifetime to lifetime until I was evolved enough in self-consciousness to sense that there was more to life than what I experienced with my five senses. This culminated in my lifetime in ancient Greece when I had an irrepressible longing to know the meaning and purpose of life, which is why I sought out the mystic philosopher Pythagoras.

I sailed to Italy where Pythagoras resided because I had heard rumors in Athens that he was in possession of a secret knowledge of life, and I became his student for eight years before returning to Athens to take my place in the political life that I had been groomed for; and the next time I made contact with the secret knowledge of life was in Palestine during the time of Jesus. I studied the secret knowledge with the Essenes, but I did not solve the mystery of the self then, nor in my lifetime as a Sufi in Persia in the mid 15th Century; that did not happen until I made contact with the secret knowledge with Gurdjieff's teaching in my current lifetime, which awakened me to the Word.

The Word is the Way and omniscient guiding force of life that Jesus called the kingdom of heaven. "When they (his disciples) asked again, "When will the kingdom come?" Jesus replied, *"It will not come by waiting for it. It will not be a matter of saying, 'Here it is,' or 'There it is.' Rather, the kingdom of the Father is spread out upon the earth, and people do not see it"* (Gospel of Thomas). The kingdom of heaven is both the Way and a state of higher consciousness. It is the secret knowledge of life.

Once I awakened to the Way I began to see it everywhere, especially in the cryptic sayings of Jesus and in everyday life. This is how I came to see that coincidences are the Voice of God calling us to our true self. But to understand what this means I have to explain the mystery of our personal karmic destiny and our pre-ordained spiritual destiny.

As an atom of God, I was a Soul seed genetically encoded to realize my divine essence, and I was teleologically driven to evolve through life (which I later realized was life's natural impulse to individuate the Soul of life); and as I evolved from one life form to a higher life form I took in the life force, which is Divine Spirit.

The life force is the un-self-realized "I" of Soul, and the divine purpose of life is to evolve the individuating consciousness of Soul through life until it gives birth to a new "I" of God. This is how God grows in the consciousness of God. As the atom of God evolves through life it takes in the life force and individuates Soul through its particular life organism, like a rose seed individuating into a beautiful rose, a tomato seed individuating into a ripe tomato, and an acorn seed individuating into an oak tree; and the atom of God evolves up the ladder of life until it has individuated enough Soul consciousness to become aware of itself, as I did in my higher primate lifetime.

I experienced the birth of a new "I" of God in my past-life regression, and from the moment I gave birth to my reflective self-consciousness I separated from the collective consciousness of my clan and was free to make personal choices, which was the beginning of my personal karmic destiny that was distinct from the karmic destiny of my clan.

Karma is the law of harmony. It determines how the positive and negative aspects of life are kept in balance as the atom of God evolves through life. Karma is Spirit in action, and from one life to the next the atom of God is governed by the corrective karmic nature of Divine Spirit—which is the natural way of life. In effect, we have no choice but to align our personal karmic destiny with our pre-scripted spiritual destiny, because if we don't the inherently corrective nature of the process of karmic resolution will align it for us.

Karma is our personal relationship with life, and until we learn that we are the authors of our own destiny we will never break free of the hold that life has over us. But nature can only evolve us so far through the natural process of karmic resolution (creating and resolving karma from one life to the next), and then we have to take evolution into our own hands to realize our spiritual destiny. This means bringing our personal destiny into alignment with our pre-ordained spiritual destiny, which the omniscient guiding force of life is forever helping us do as Hopcke tells us in *There Are No Accidents: Synchronicities and the Stories of Our Lives.* He gives us many examples of how people found their path and grew in their wholeness through synchronicity; some so amazing that they bordered on divine intervention—which for me is what they are, anyway.

If I may then, let me relate my unbelievable experience of divine intervention. I've had many, but this one still makes me shake my head in absolute wonder. Penny and I wanted to relocate to South Central Ontario for reasons that would require a whole book to explain, and we decided to get a mortgage on our triplex in my hometown of Nipigon and build a new house in Georgian Bay. Penny said to me on the morning I left to drive to Georgian Bay to look for a building lot, "Please find us a nice lot for our new home."

She didn't know it, but she put a lot of pressure on me, and I couldn't disappoint her after what I had put her through; so I asked God to give me a sign which lot to buy.

I was adamant in my request. "I don't want just any sign," I said to God. "I want an unequivocal sign or none at all." My back was to the wall because of the book I had just published (*What Would I Say Today If I Were To Die Tomorrow?*). My novel exposed the shadow side of my hometown personality, and Penny's co-workers in the hospital office made her life so unbearable because of my novel that we decided it was best to relocate.

After looking at building lots in the communities of Meaford, Thornbury, and Wasaga that just didn't feel right, Penny's friend from Wasaga, who was helping me look for a lot because his son was going to build our new house, said that a contractor friend of his had heard of some building lots in Tiny Beaches; so we drove there, and to my absolute astonishment we came upon a street called STOCCO CIRCLE in an area called Bluewater. Stocco is my last name, and "O" is my nickname—*Stocco Circle!*

"Please God, let there be a lot for sale on this street," I silently pleaded; and there was only one lot for sale on STOCCO CIRCLE that I later learned had gone up for sale on the same day that I asked God to give me a sign for the right lot to buy for our new home, and I was the first person to bid on it; and, to put icing on the cake, it was five thousand dollars below our allotted building lot budget!

Needless to say we built our new house on STOCCO CIRCLE, the street with my name; and after living in Bluewater for three years Penny said to me: "Of all the places down here, I wouldn't trade where we live for any one of them. I love where we live."

"Thank you, God," I said, and have thanked God every day since.

"We come into life as sparks of divine consciousness," I told Carl Jung in my dream, "and our purpose in life is to evolve in self-consciousness until we realize our divine essence, which you pointed to with your understanding of the individuation process. To answer your question on the alpha and omega of the self, then; we all begin as un-self-realized atoms of God, and we evolve through the life process to acquire our own individual identity; and we return to God fully self-realized, God-conscious Souls—which means that total self-realization consciousness is the fundamental purpose of life, just as you intuited in your memoir *Memories, Dreams, Reflections*."

The day after my dream I looked up the passage that I referenced where Jung had captured the central archetype of the Self (the divinely encoded atom of God) that drives the entire process of individuation: "Unconscious wholeness therefore seems to me the true *spiritus rector* of all biological and psychic events. Here is a principle which strives for total realization—which in man's case signifies the attainment of total consciousness. Attainment of consciousness is culture in the broadest sense, and self-knowledge is therefore the heart and essence of this process" (*Memories, Dreams, Reflections*, p. 324). I smiled upon reading this, because Jung had the answer all along but hadn't connected all the dots.

"Know thyself," said the Oracle of Delphi, upon which my favorite philosopher Socrates built his teaching of self-realization consciousness, and I spent my whole life examining my life; but little did I expect that I would be reborn into my same life over again to obtain a different outcome, as St. Padre Pio said I did. This takes self-examination to a whole new level, and I can't wait to see what I uncover with *The Summoning of Noman*—"Noman," of course, being the archetypal shadow self that kept me from finding my true self the first time I lived my life as Orest Stocco. But I can't help wondering if this book isn't already published over there also…

10. Prisoners of Our Own Vanity

Gurdjieff said: "If a man in prison was at any time to have a chance to escape, then he must first of all *realize that he is in prison.* So long as he fails to realize this, so long as he thinks he is free, he has no chance whatever. No one can help or liberate him by force, against his will, in opposition to his wishes. If liberation is possible, it is possible only as a result of great labor and great effort, and, above all, of conscious efforts, towards a definite aim." (*In Search of the Miraculous,* P. D. Ouspensky, p. 30)

I was in prison, but I didn't realize it until I went to a very gifted intuitive empath for the spiritual healing that became the basis of my novel *Healing with Padre Pio*. My prison was my own vanity, and not until I experienced the devastating power of St. Padre Pio's humility did I see the proud shadow face of my spiritual conceit. I could not believe that it was me, and I wanted to throw up in disgust!

I had come a long way since I discovered Gurdjieff at university when a fellow philosophy student, for whatever reason (I have since come to believe that he was guided by Divine Spirit) gave me a copy of Ouspensky's book *In Search of the Miraculous*. "I think you'll find this book interesting," he said when he returned after the Christmas break, little realizing that it would dramatically change the course of my entire life.

Gurdjieff fascinated me from the moment his former student Ouspensky introduced the enigmatic teacher to the world in his remarkable memoir *In Search of the Miraculous*, and he continued to fascinate me for years as I "worked" on myself with his teaching of self-transformation; and I give Gurdjieff full credit for helping me break out of the prison of my unconscious false personality.

The more I "worked" on myself with Gurdjieff's teaching, the more I awakened to the Word, the omniscient guiding force of life that has been called the Way throughout recorded history; and I became omnivorous in my appetite for the Way, which I began to see everywhere. Eventually I came to the realization that life *is* the Way, and that all spiritual paths are different expressions of the Way specifically suited to the stages of one's journey through life, or one's particular level of consciousness if you will.

And the more I *lived* the principles of the Way (especially the sayings of Jesus), the more I transformed my consciousness until one fine day the divine law of synchronicity introduced me to what St. Padre Pio called "that other religion" that I was closed-minded about the first time I lived my life as Orest Stocco. This time around however I took to the Way of the Eternal and have been living it for the past thirty years.

"I'm home!" I exclaimed, when I read the book that introduced me to the Way of the Eternal, so much did it resonate with my new state of consciousness; and I committed myself to this teaching for the rest of my life never expecting that one day I would anticipate leaving it because I would trap myself by the false sense of spiritual security that this ancient spiritual teaching gave me.

In all fairness, it wasn't the Way of the Eternal that had trapped me; it was the vanity that "the most direct path to God" fosters with the false sense of spiritual security that it affords its followers, especially High Initiates; but I would never have realized that I had become a prisoner of my own vanity had I not gone for a spiritual healing with St. Padre Pio. He slew the vanity of my spiritual conceit with the redemptive love of his infinite compassion and woke me up to the distorted reality of my situation; and shortly after I brought my novel *Healing with Padre Pio* to closure I had the following dream:

I was on the train that had just pulled out of the station platform of what I knew to be my spiritual community. I had just gotten on the train and was staring out the window. The grounds of my community were impeccably kept, beautiful lush green lawns, flowers, trees, shrubbery, and a beautiful small lake with benches here and there; and the building was made of stone with beautiful arched windows and doors, and it covered a large part of the community grounds; but as the train pulled away from the community grounds I got the feeling from some of the members watching the train go by that they couldn't understand why I was leaving. But as beautiful and safe and secure as our spiritual community was, I couldn't help but feel that we were all prisoners of the shadow personality of our spiritual community, and it was time to move on. I felt sad for leaving, but I was also relieved that I had finally made the decision to leave our community prison of spiritual freedom.

I trust my dreams because dreams don't lie. Dreams are messages from Soul to the conscious mind, and my dream was telling me that it was time to move on. Curiously enough, a month or so after this dream I got confirmation from another dream that my spiritual community was under the hypnotic spell of its shadow personality:

I was in a large hall where the spiritual leader of the Way of the Eternal was going to give a talk. I was standing at the back of the stage watching everyone come into the room and take a seat. I could see that every chela that came into the room was under the hypnotic spell of the false sense of spiritual security that the Way of the Eternal gave them. When everyone was seated the Inner Master walked up to the podium. Dressed in his customary blue suit, he looked out at the audience, and without saying a word he snapped the fingers of his right hand and everyone woke up from the hypnotic spell that they were under.

My dream confirmed that I was no longer under the hypnotic spell that the Way of the Eternal fosters with its promise of spiritual security with initiations to the Higher Planes of Consciousness; but what exactly is this false sense of spiritual security?

Walking down the street of a large urban center, a smartly dressed woman is approached by a wide-eyed bearded man holding some pamphlets who announces, "Have you been saved?"

The smartly dressed woman replies, "Thank you, but I'm not interested."

"Jesus died on the cross for your sins—"

The woman walks away, not wanting to be bothered, and the evangelical Christian approaches other pedestrians with the same passionate zeal to save their soul; but he gets rebuffed again and again. Still, he continues accosting pedestrians because he believes that Jesus sacrificed his life on the cross for the salvation of the world.

This is an extreme example (imagined, but not uncommon) of the power of blind belief; and although it does not come across like this in the spiritual path that I embraced after I moved on from

STUPIDITY IS NOT A GIFT OF GOD

Gurdjieff's teaching, the Way of the Eternal is no less persuasive—if not dangerously more so, as I rudely came to realize.

All Christians breathe the same air. They grow up believing that Jesus is the savior of the world. But depending upon life and circumstances, some Christians step outside their spiritual paradigm and see that God's mercy blesses everyone equally. That happened to me when I stepped outside the paradigm of the Way of the Eternal for the novel that I was inspired to write on the mysterious phenomenon of spiritual healing.

I went to a gifted empath for a spiritual healing, and her guide, the Ascended Master St. Padre Pio, slew the vanity of my spiritual conceit and woke me up to the reality that no path to God was more valid than another, and it was arrogant to believe otherwise.

Like every Initiate of the Way of the Eternal (especially High Initiates, myself included), I grew to believe that our spiritual path was not only the most direct path to God, but the most exclusive because our spiritual leader embodied the highest manifestation of God-realization consciousness in all the worlds, both inner and outer, who not only initiated us into the Holy Current of God that flows through life, but who also came to us in our dreams to teach us the secret knowledge of the Way of the Eternal—an elitist *shadow conviction* held by our whole community but which no one dared to raise to a conscious level of awareness, just as Christians have done with their brazen *shadow conviction* that only through Jesus Christ can we be saved. This is what nurtured my spiritual conceit.

And this is why I brought *Healing with Padre Pio* to closure with the chapter "The Vanity of All Spiritual Paths," because no path (including the Way of the Eternal) is exempt from the infinitely seductive power of the mind that traps us all in the comfortable prison of our own vanity, which is why St. Padre Pio told me that life is all about GROWTH and UNDERSTANDING—a humbling journey of the self through vanity to humility. As the Preacher said long ago, *"vanity of vanities; all is vanity. What profit hath a man of all his labor which he taketh under the sun?"*

The answer to this question is going to be the theme of the next book that I'm going to work on with the Ascended Master, and I can't wait to write it.

PART TWO

"People are frightened to find out who they really are, for when they know that completely, they feel the responsibility is too great."

THE ONLY PLANET OF CHOICE
Phyllis Schlemer

11. Trust God, but Don't Forget To Flush the Toilet

"Did you have diarrhea?" Penny queried, poking her head into my den. I was deep in thought on my musing "Prisoners of Our Own Vanity."

"A bit," I replied. "Did I forget to flush the toilet?"

"No; but I had to flush it again and clean it," she said.

"I'm sorry, love. I didn't look to check. I'm caught up in my musing."

"I know," she said, with great understanding.

"I apologize. I should have checked." I felt foolish and embarrassed that she had to clean up after me; and then, to my surprise, the words just leapt out of my mouth— *'trust God, but don't forget to flush the toilet!'* And I broke into laughter. "This is what my new book of spiritual musings is all about," I added, still chuckling. After all, it was my responsibility to see to it that the toilet was flushed clean when I was done."

"I know; but we're a team," she said, smiling at me as she always does whenever I erupt into laughter at my spontaneous epiphanies.

"Still, it was my responsibility. It won't happen again," I said.

When I erupted with *"trust God, but don't forget to flush the toilet,"* which my Muse gave me to capture the aphoristic wisdom of my embarrassing experience, my creative unconscious was playing upon the Sufi saying *"trust Allah, but tie up your camel,"* and I knew instantly that I had to do a spiritual musing on this saying—especially since this was the second time that this title had popped into my mind; but where to start?

Once again, I abandoned to my Muse…

I'm deep into research on C. G. Jung for my new book *The Summoning of Noman,* and I just finished reading *Jung and the Story of Our Time*, by Laurens van der Post, a personal and intimate portrait of the eminent Swiss psychologist whose life and teaching have become an inspiration for countless people throughout the world, and it was Jung's conviction—if I may express it in the humorous context of my new saying *trust God but don't forget to flush the toilet*—that man is ultimately responsible for his own salvation.

Laurens van der Post writes: "The messages to the churches and temples of the day was clear; they were emptying fast because they had defaulted on their mission of enabling man to become new and whole, and would empty altogether and crumble unless they returned to healing in a contemporary way leading to an achievement or wholeness in a twentieth-century context. And none of this healing was possible except by facing honestly and with the utmost courage the problem of the shadow cast not only by man in himself but by God on life." (*Jung and the Story of Our Time*, p. 219)

This was Jung's belief: unless man comes to terms with his own shadow he will never realize singleness and wholeness of self; and by shadow he meant the dark, repressed repository of everything that we refuse to integrate into our conscious personality. In a word, **our shadow is who we don't want to be.**

But we cannot be what we are destined to become unless we transform the consciousness of our shadow and become one whole, integrated self—which Jesus called "salvation" and Jung, speaking for modern man, called "individuation process."

When Jesus talked about dying to our life to save our life (**"He that loveth his life shall lose it; and he that hateth his life in this world shall keep it unto life eternal"** John 12: 25), he was talking about transforming the consciousness of our shadow; but Christ's Way of self-sacrifice has lost its resonance with modern man, and this puzzles us.

"The future of mankind very much depends upon the recognition of the shadow," said Jung in a letter to Father Victor White. "Evil is—psychologically speaking—*terribly real.*" (*Jung and the Story of Our Time*, p. 223)

Evil is not a privation of good, as my old Roman Catholic faith believes—a doctrine that Carl Jung found odious in light of his research on the psyche of man; it is the reality of the shadow, personal and collective.

STUPIDITY IS NOT A GIFT OF GOD

"My name is legion," said Satan; but for the life of me, I cannot see why society refuses to acknowledge the disastrous effects of our collective shadow personality.

We experience these ghoulish forces daily by way of social unrest, economic and political disruptions, and environmental disasters (*"Nature patterns after man, not man after nature,"* said Philos the Tibetan, which Jung amplifies with Richard Wilhelm's story of the rainmaker who brought rain to the village that was out of harmony with the Tao); but we fail to make the connection between individual choices and collective consequences—*as though personal karma operated in a void!* Has rational self-interest spiritually blinded modern man? Is that the source of our problems today?

Everything seems to point to society's karmic obtuseness, and I'm afraid the only way out is through the horns of our spiritual dilemma. In short, we can trust God all we want; but we must never forget to flush the toilet!

12. Is Jesus Christ Relevant Today

I've been plagued by a thought lately that I just can't seem to get out of my mind—that Jesus Christ is no longer relevant today; and I know that the only way I can come to terms with this thought is to do a spiritual musing on it.

As always, whenever I'm called to do a spiritual musing I have to have an entry point; and just as I decided to do a spiritual musing on whether or not Jesus Christ is relevant today my Muse whispered into my ear, *"The inherently self-correcting nature of life,"* and I caught a fleeting glimpse of where I have to go to resolve the issue of Jesus Christ's relevance to the modern world...

I've just finished another edit of my novel *Jesus Wears Dockers, The Gospel Conspiracy Story,* which was my inspired effort to decode the cryptic sayings of Jesus; and as I thought about the entry point that my Muse gave me for today's spiritual musing, I realized that *Jesus Wears Dockers* creatively transforms reality into a deeper perception of what is and confirms the inherently self-correcting nature of life.

It may take a long time, centuries even, but however long it takes the false structures of human thought will eventually collapse from the pressures of reality; that's what happens to a belief system that cannot support the insufferable weight of its own falseness—like political belief systems that suppress man's inherent need for individual expression.

It's all about boxes; mental boxes that refuse to expand and allow for the natural unfoldment of human consciousness—both individually and socially. And unless these mental boxes expand to allow for the evolution of human consciousness, the pressure will cause all kinds of pain and suffering; hence the Arab Spring, for example.

State dictatorships are no less oppressive and restricting to individual growth than a marital relationship where a husband controls his wife and keeps her from growing into the person she is meant to be; it will cause cracks in the relationship and something will have to give, be it a social revolution or divorce.

That happened to me. My Roman Catholic faith was too constricting for my irrepressible need to be myself; that's why I left my faith and became a seeker. And I found the path that would take me to my true self. But ironically the path that I found included the secret Way of Christ. That's what inspired my novel *Jesus Wears Dockers,* and why I believe this was nature's way (my creative unconscious) of correcting my life—because my faith had created a box of beliefs that could not contain me, and I could not breathe.

My faith held that my soul was created at the moment of my human conception, that I only lived one lifetime, and that Jesus was the one and only true savior of the world; but my personal experiences contradicted my faith, and I suffered unbearable anguish.

When I discovered Darwin and natural evolution at the age of fifteen, my parish priest patted me on the head and told me not to worry my head over that stuff; we were born of Adam and Eve, and that was that. And when I discovered reincarnation shortly after, he said the same thing; but that did not satisfy my need to know, and I became a seeker.

I had to find proof that I lived more than one lifetime and that there was more than one way to salvation; and after years of searching Gurdjieff came into my life, and his teaching of "work on oneself" awakened me to the Word within, which Jesus called the "water of everlasting life." That's how I found the secret Way of Christ in the sayings of Jesus, which many years later led to my novel *Jesus Wears Dockers* that dispelled "the Gospel conspiracy" and corrected the Christian message.

The Christian message states that we only live one life and that Jesus died on the cross to save us from eternal damnation. This is not the case. Soul, our immortal spiritual essence, pre-exists our mortal human life; and through the natural process of human evolution our spiritual essence evolves through many incarnations until we realize that we are individual expressions of God divinely encoded to become spiritually self-realized, God conscious Souls; and the real message of Jesus teaches us how to do this.

That's what my novel *Jesus Wears Dockers* is all about, and why I believe my Muse inspired the thought that my novel is nature's way of correcting my life; but how does this answer the question, *is Jesus Christ relevant today?*

All the research that I've been doing for *The Summoning of Noman* has opened me up to the expansive world of the worldwide web, and I cannot believe the number of people out there whose life experiences shatter old paradigms and allow the spirit of man to breathe freely for the first time in centuries; but because we are free to choose the life we live we can consciously participate in the expansion of world consciousness, or we can suffer the indignity of being dragged by it. This is why I titled this volume of spiritual musings *Stupidity is Not a Gift of God*—because man continually chooses to be dragged by his own destiny and then blames God (or whatever) for his suffering.

We can choose to believe that we only live one life and that Jesus is the only savior of the world, or we can step outside this little box and experience the vast expanses of our spiritual nature in the knowledge that we are Soul and that our purpose in life is to grow and evolve into our true self and become co-creators with God; it's always our choice.

Anita Moorjani, author of *Dying To Be Me*: *My Journey From Cancer, to Near Death, to True Healing* had an NDE and was told on the other side to return to her body and share her healing experience with the world; and Doctor Jeffrey Long, author of *Evidence of the Afterlife*, has researched thousands of NDEs and has shattered the old scientific paradigm that there is no life after death; and Dolores Cannon, who has regressed thousands of people to their past lives and retrieved invaluable information that parts the veiled curtains of life, as has Dr. Brian L. Weiss, author of *Many Lives, Many Masters*; and neurosurgeon Dr. Ebin Alexander, who was stuck in his scientific paradigm, records his "perfect storm" out-of-body experience in his book *Proof of Heaven*; and on and on—a countless number of people today whose personal experiences are expanding human consciousness and allowing the soul of man to breathe in the refreshing air of spiritual enlightenment as never before in the history of the world.

So, is Jesus Christ relevant or not today?

STUPIDITY IS NOT A GIFT OF GOD

      The answer is YES and NO. Jesus is no longer relevant to the modern world as long as we keep him locked up in the box that Christianity has put him in; and he is relevant when we listen to the original message that he gave to the world on how to realize our destiny to spiritual self-realization consciousness. That's why I wrote my dialectical novel *Jesus Wears Dockers*, *The Gospel Conspiracy Story*—to take Jesus out of that suffocating little box that Christianity has put him in and set him free.

13. A Very Strange Virus

It's a very strange virus. It's everywhere and cannot be destroyed. It lays dormant in life, and it only strikes certain people; and when it strikes it changes your life.

"He's gone religious," they say, when one catches this virus; and out of fear of being contaminated by this strange virus one's family keeps its distance and makes apologies for you, and your friends begin to drop away one by one.

I caught this strange virus in high school. The contagion was Somerset Maugham's novel *The Razor's Edge*. Maugham's hero Larry Darrel, a former World War I aviator who was haunted by the death of his friend that was killed saving his life, goes on a quest for the meaning and purpose of life. So moved was I by Larry Darrel that he infected me with the strange virus and I became a spiritual seeker also.

For reasons which took years to understand (long after I found my own answer to the meaning and purpose of life), I finally figured out why this strange virus affects some people and not others; and that's the subject of today's spiritual musing…

If, as I have come to believe, we are all born with a seed of divine consciousness that is encoded to become spiritually self-realized and God conscious, and the purpose of life is to evolve this seed of divine consciousness, then our life *has* inherent purpose; but ironically we are not conscious of our purpose, which is why we question the meaning of life.

But what if, as I have also come to believe, life is driven by an omniscient guiding intelligence, and this intelligence directs the evolution of life until we sense our inherent purpose, it would explain why we have this need to know the meaning of life.

This is the human condition. We are here to grow and evolve until we realize the inherent potential of our divine nature, and had I not experienced what I did in one of my past-life regressions all of this would be fatuous speculation.

STUPIDITY IS NOT A GIFT OF GOD

In my regression I was brought back to the Body of God where all seeds of divine consciousness originate. I did not have self-consciousness. From the perspective of my evolved self that was brought back to the origins of my life in the Body of God, I could see that I was a soul without a reflective self; and in the same regression I was brought back to my first human lifetime as a higher primate when I gave birth to my reflective self-consciousness, and with each subsequent incarnation I grew in the consciousness of my reflective human self through the process of natural evolution.

Once I experienced myself as an un-self-realized seed of divine consciousness that evolved through life until I gave birth to my reflective self-consciousness, I began to piece together the puzzle of life; and when I connected the dots of my past-life regressions with my gnosis of the Way I caught my first glimpse of the purpose of life, which is to expand the consciousness of God through the evolution of life.

Quite simply, the seeds of divine consciousness are planted in the world to evolve until they give birth to a new "I" of God—a reflective self-consciousness. When the seed of divine consciousness has given birth to its reflective self it creates personal karma, which is born of personal choice; and with each new incarnation the "I" of God grows in self-realization consciousness through the natural process of karmic reconciliation until it is ready to take evolution into its own hands and realize its inherent purpose.

Unfortunately nature cannot evolve the seed of divine consciousness beyond a certain point, because life is made up of the consciousness of being and becoming, which is the consciousness of life and death; and to evolve in spiritual self-realization consciousness we have to take evolution into our own hands and transform the consciousness of our human self. This is why teachers like Jesus come into the world; they introduce us to the Way, which is the path to spiritual self-realization and God consciousness.

My introduction to the Way was through Gurdjieff's teaching; but I would not have found Gurdjieff had I not been infected by that strange virus in high school. The virus compelled me to become a seeker like Larry Darrel, and Gurdjieff's teaching awakened me to the Way; and the more conscious I became of the Way by "working" on myself with G's teaching, the more I was attracted to teachers of the Way—like Jesus.

Jesus was the Way incarnate. ***"I am the way, the truth, and the life,"*** said Jesus; so I took his sayings to heart and made them central to my path. And that's when the virus really took hold of me and I became feverish with the Way. ***"He that findeth his life shall lose it; and he that loseth his life for my sake shall find it,"*** said Jesus; and I "died" daily to my life as I lived the Way with pathological commitment.

My family was worried about me. "You change before my eyes," my mother said to me when my fever was dangerously high; but I was so caught up in my search for my true self that nothing could stop me from "dying" to my life to "find" my life; and the only cure to my infection was spiritual self-realization consciousness, which I experienced one day in my mother's kitchen while she was kneading bread dough on the kitchen table.

After I gave "birth" to my spiritual self (to use Jesus' terminology for shifting my center of gravity from my lower to higher self), I began to find some balance in my life; and my family began to ease off, but not entirely. I was still strange to them.

And then something even stranger happened. My fever spiked again and I became so feverish that I was pulled into the strange world of an offshoot Christian solar cult teaching that threw my life into chaos, and it took years to make peace with my decision to study this teaching that did irreparable damage to my eyesight.

I did not know that it was a false teaching of Light, that's why it was so traumatizing; but for past-life reasons I had to experience what I did with this teaching to balance out my karmic account, and one day I will write a novel about this soul-wrenching experience. My Muse has already supplied me with the title: "The Sunworshipper."

My fever went away after this experience, and I began to find some balance again in my life; and from day to day I lived the Way of the Eternal (the spiritual path that Gurdjieff's teaching had prepared me for) until I met Penny and we got together.

And then I wrote a novel (*What Would I Say Today If I Were To Die Tomorrow?*) that so disturbed the shadow personality of my hometown that Penny and I relocated to Georgian Bay, South Central

Ontario; so I know what it means to be infected by this strange virus, because I was infected by it from the day I met Larry Darrel in grade twelve.

Maugham introduced his novel with a saying from the Upanishads that reflects how dangerous this virus can be: *"The sharp edge of the razor is difficult to walk over; thus the wise say the road to salvation is hard."* Larry Darrel walked the razor's edge, and so did I; he found his peace, and so did I; and now I can reveal the mystery of why only some people and not others are infected by this strange virus…

"To everything there is a season, and a time to every purpose under the heaven," said the Preacher in *Ecclesiastes*; and so it is with personal salvation. As strange as this may sound, not everyone is ready to be saved, and by saved I mean ready to take evolution into one's own hands to realize one's divine purpose in life.

I was ready. That's why I was infected by this strange virus. But why does this virus only affect those who are ready for the Way? Jesus said, **"Many are called, but few are chosen,"** but what makes some people ready to be chosen and not others?

This has puzzled the world for centuries, and only mystics like St. Teresa of Avila understand this mystery (her book *Interior Castle* infected Carolyn Myss, who wrote *Entering the Castle* that puts St. Teresa's message into a modern context)*;* and St. Padre Pio, who was so infected by this virus that he suffered the stigmata for fifty years. So what is it about this strange virus that it can possess our soul with such feverish intensity?

I've given this a lot of thought over the years, but not until I connected some very elusive dots did I see what this strange virus was and why it only infects some people and not others; and this speaks directly to *quantum spirituality post 2012*.

I had to connect three dots to create a perspective large enough to see into the heart of the Divine Matrix, as it were; but I did not connect these three dots all at once. I connected the first two dots, and then I connected the third dot and saw the big picture.

The first dot is *creative life force*. The second dot is *consciousness.* And the third dot is *Divine Spirit.* Science has shown that all life forms have consciousness, but what is consciousness if not the creative life force? That's the question I asked myself. But rather than commit myself to a life-long study to prove this (which may take quantum physics a hundred years yet to prove), I just accepted what I intuited to be true; and this allowed me to connect the third dot of **Divine Spirit** which, with Gurdjieff's teaching of "work on oneself" and Christ's sayings, I experienced to be the living Word that spoke the Way.

"In the beginning was the Word, and the Word was with God, and the Word was God," said St. John. This is very mystical and hard to conceptualize, because the Word has to be experienced to be appreciated (which is why Jesus said that his teaching was for those that had eyes to see and ears to hear); but when all is said and done, **Divine Spirit** is the contagion that infects us with the salvation virus when we are ready to take evolution into our own hands and realize our divine purpose.

This is how the dynamics of life work: we need the life force to grow and evolve. The life force is the consciousness of life, so the more life force we take in the more we individuate the consciousness of life and grow in self-realization consciousness; but because the life force is a consciousness of *being* and *becoming* (life and death), we can never realize our spiritual nature (or give birth to our spiritual self, as Jesus would say) because our human self-consciousness is not pure enough to realize our divine nature.

We have to refine the consciousness of our life to realize our divine nature; and we can only do that by taking evolution into our own hands. And we can only do that when we are evolved enough to see that the karma that we create keeps us trapped in the recurring cycle of *being* and *becoming* — meaning, the endless cycle of life and death.

We are ready to be saved then when the natural process of evolution through karma and reincarnation has evolved us to the point where we can see that we are responsible for the life that we create because of the choices we make, and not until we take responsibility for our own karma can we change our life and break the cycle of life and death; and when we are ready to take responsibility for our own life Divine Spirit infects us with the salvation virus and we become spiritual seekers like my high school hero Larry Darrel.

Larry was ready to be saved, but he had to be infected by the salvation virus to take evolution into his own hands. Divine Spirit, the omniscient guiding force of life infected him when his friend sacrificed his life to save his, which threw Larry into a spiritual crisis that compelled him to become a spiritual seeker; and Larry's commitment to find the answer to the riddle of life was so contagious that I caught the virus from him and went on my own spiritual quest. But I was only infected because I was ready.

I was ready because of my past lives, which I explore in my novel *Cathedral of My Past Lives*; and I was called by the omniscient guiding force of life to break the karmic cycle of my spiritual life, and I heeded the call when I read *The Razor's Edge*.

Not everyone who hears the call heeds it; but in the Divine Plan of God there is no time limit, and we will just keep coming back until we are ready. This is why some people are infected by this strange virus and not others.

14. Who's Driving Your Bus Today?

"Man has no individuality. He has no single, big I. Man is divided into a multiplicity of small I's. And each separate small I is able to call itself by the name of the Whole, to act in the name of the Whole, to agree or disagree, to give promises, to make decisions with which another I, or the Whole will have to deal. This explains why people so often make decisions and so seldom carry them out..." (*In Search of the Miraculous*, p. 60).

When I first came upon this concept of multiple I's in Gurdjieff's teaching it was like I had stepped into the secret world of the human psyche, and I stood frozen at the mystery of the self of man; and like a deer frozen by the headlights of an oncoming vehicle, I stood dazed by the light that Gurdjieff had just shone into the secret chambers of my psyche, and I felt a mixture of terror, excitement, and relief. *"Finally,"* I managed to say; *"someone who understands my situation!"*

I knew that I was a multiplicity of I's, but I could never acknowledge this awareness consciously; it was like a terrifying secret that I kept from myself. This was another reason why Gurdjieff pulled me into his teaching, and this concept of multiple I's fueled my desire to integrate myself into one single, whole self; but that was a long time coming.

Gurdjieff had a "system" to integrate my multiple I's. Perhaps this is why he called his teaching "the System," among other names like "the Work," "the Fourth Way," and my favorite name "the way of the sly man." This became my favorite name only when I initiated myself into the secret way of the sly man, which perhaps I can explore in another musing. In today's spiritual musing I want to explore the mystery of multiple I's...

I wish I could take credit for the image that captures this concept of multiple I's with the kind of genius that only symbolic imagery can capture, but I have to give credit to Patti Simpson, the author of *Paulji: A Memoir,* where I discovered it; and Patti credits a man called Jim, whom she met in Tahiti where she went for a much needed vacation after the death of her husband. On the island of Bora Bora, Patti became friends with Jim, a young attorney from San Diego, California. She enjoyed his company, and especially his whacky sense of humor which helped her through her grieving period.

They were both guests of a private club and met every mealtime at community tables, and each morning at breakfast Jim would regale Patti with his romantic misadventures of the previous evening. One morning he arrived at the table looking a little rough around the edges, and Patti inquired how his evening went. He rolled his eyes and sighed. "You wouldn't believe it," he said.

"Try me," Patti said, and laughed.

"Well," he said, "in order to understand what happened, I have to introduce you to my bus. You see, I am not really one individual. I am a busload of individuals, and who I am and what I do depends upon who's driving my bus at any given moment."

Patti was intrigued, so she pressed Jim for details; and it turns out that Jim had met the most beautiful creature he had ever seen. She was gorgeous, and she liked him, and they danced several times and he felt something good was going to come out of it and asked if she would like a drink. She said yes, so he went to the bar and ordered a drink for both; but while waiting for his drinks he met an Australian and struck up a conversation.

The Australian said that there wasn't an American alive who could hold a candle to the Australians when it came to drinking, thus throwing down the gauntlet; and Jim, of course, wasn't going to take the challenge because he had a beautiful woman waiting for him, but before he knew it "the Midnight Rider slipped in and said, 'I can handle this one,' and he was in the driver's seat." And the rest...well, you can imagine what happened.

Jim lost both the challenge and the prospect of a wonderful evening with a gorgeous woman, and quite possibly the most beautiful romance of his life; and all because "Romantic Jim" had to forfeit the driver's seat of his bus to the "Midnight Rider" who had to defend the honor of the American male ego—which proves what Gurdjieff said about one I making a decision and another I failing to see it through...

This was my challenge with Gurdjieff's teaching, to make one single I out of my multiplicity of I's, and my salvation was what Gurdjieff called a "Work" I. A "Work" I was the I that I created as I "worked" on myself with Gurdjieff's transformative techniques of *non-identification, self-remembering, voluntary effort*, and *conscious suffering*.

One could call this "Work" I a unifying principle that integrates one's many I's, which is not restricted to Gurdjieff's teaching alone because a unifying principle can be created out of any discipline in life, like living a Socratic life of virtue, for example—which, incidentally, I also employed to integrate myself into one single, harmonious I; or living the sayings of Jesus, which I also employed in my efforts to integrate my many I's; or long distance running, which I also used as a unifying principle to integrate myself.

"In running I found my salvation," said Dr. George Sheehan, who was called "the guru of running." He couldn't explain why running was his salvation, but he knew that running fulfilled his life, and he ran until his body no longer permitted him to run; but he died satisfied in his efforts to live a whole, complete life; and I thank Dr. George Sheehan's book *Running and Being* for the inspiration it gave me to take up running.

I wrote my own book on running called *Thoughts in Motion: Diary of a Holistic Runner,* which is waiting patiently for my attention in one of my boxes of manuscripts in the basement of our new house here in Georgian Bay, and I'd like to share one dream from this unpublished manuscript that I had one night which will explain in one incredible image the mystery of the unifying, integrative principle of running.

Dreams are messages from the unconscious that speak in a language that transcends thoughts and words. Dreams speak in symbols, and symbols speak for the whole Self; which makes dream symbols so rich in meaning that one dream can take a person a lifetime to decipher; for example, Frank N. McMillan Jr., "a country boy steeped in the traditional culture of rural Texas who was summoned to a life-long quest for meaning by a dream lion he met in the night" (*Finding Jung, A Life in Quest of the Lion,* Frank. N. McMillan III); and Carl Jung, the world's foremost interpreter of dreams, had symbolic dreams in his youth that did not reveal their meaning until late in life. I've also had dreams that didn't give up their meaning for years; but fortunately I decoded the message of my running dream, and I marvel at how brilliant it was in explaining how running became my "salvation."

    I learned from Jung that to understand a dream we have to see it in the context of one's life, especially in the context that gave birth to the dream; and the context that gave birth to the symbol of my running dream was this: I was deep into Gurdjieff's teaching of "work on oneself," and I was living the sayings of Jesus, plus I had incorporated into my personal path dozens of wisdom sayings that I read three times every morning before I started my work day. My vocation was contract painting, plus I steam cleaned carpets to supplement my income, and I packed these wisdom sayings into my "Work" self and took on my day with Gurdjieffian gusto. I did this for a number of years, and then I was nudged to take up long distance running which wasn't easy getting into; but I knew that this was going to be good for me, and I read all I could on running (Valerie Andrew's book *The Psychic Power of Running* combusted my desire for running), and I bought the right shoes and togs and then found an old logging road to train before I began running along the beautiful Lake Helen shoreline where I ended up running seven miles every day for years, and ten and twelve miles a day on weekends. And then I had my dream…

    In my dream I'm running on Highway 11, along the beautiful shoreline of Lake Helen a mile or so from my hometown of Nipigon, Northwestern Ontario. As always, I began my run a few hundred yards from St. Sylvester's Historic Mission Church (where I volunteered six weeks of my time one summer to paint; another unifying principle that ensouled my "Work" I with what Jesus called "treasures in heaven" and St. Padre Pio called "glory" (the inherently self-transcending energy of goodness), and I was just getting into my run when suddenly my running dream turns symbolic and I have a ball of string in my mouth that is made up of many tiny pieces of string tied together and rolled up into a ball; and as I'm running the string is being pulled out of my mouth by an invisible hand in front of me, and the ball of string gets smaller, and smaller, and smaller; and I wake up!

I was puzzled by the dream and pondered it for days. Then one morning I'm reading my three pages of wisdom sayings as I always did before going to work to impress upon my mind how to live my life within the parameters of my "Work" I when suddenly I have a revelation: "THESE WISDOM SAYINGS ARE MY BALL OF STRING!"

In one glorious insight I connected the dots and realized that each saying that I recited ("mouthed") was connected ("tied") to the other sayings, and as I repeated these wisdom sayings three times every morning I hoped to train my subconscious to act them out throughout my day. All of my wisdom sayings were "mouthed" every morning before going to work; but the wisdom of these sayings only became mine as I *lived* them (symbolized by the act of running in my dream)—just as Jesus said about his sayings: **"Therefore whosoever heareth these sayings of mine, and <u>doeth</u> them, I will liken him unto a wise man, which buildeth his house upon a rock..."** (Math. 7:24).

By "house" Jesus meant one's "Work" I, or new state of consciousness; and by "rock" he meant one's spiritual self, and his sayings, if *lived*, would transform the consciousness of one's lower self (one's many I's) and give birth to one's spiritual self; so the miracle of Christ's teaching lies in the DOING of it; which is precisely what the symbol of my dream image was telling me.

As I ran, the wisdom sayings that I "mouthed" every morning BECAME my wisdom as long as I LIVED them in my daily life; and the more I LIVED them (the further I ran), the more they became mine and no longer needed to be "mouthed" to remind my "Work" I to LIVE them throughout the day. As the ball of string was pulled out of my mouth as I was running, I knew that the wisdom sayings would BECOME me, and I no longer would have to "mouth" them because LIVING them would become instinctive to my nature (the ball of string would eventually disappear)—which led me to the simple realization of Gurdjieff's statement that *"there is only self-initiation into the mysteries of life!"*

Once I deciphered the message of my dream image, I wanted to conceptualize my newfound realization so I could articulate it in my writing; and the more I thought about it the more meaning I got out of my dream image, until I came to the realization that the act of

DOING engendered the miracle of what Jung called the "individuation process."

But what Jung didn't realize (perhaps this is why he came to me in a dream one night to talk about my book *The Way of Soul*) was that the natural process of individuation would only take us so far in life, and no further; and to complete our destiny we have to take the natural process of individuation into our own hands and speed it up by consciously participating in our own evolution—just as Gurdjieff said we had to do; and long distance running was one other way that I took the individuation process into my own hands.

Gurdjieff said that nature would only evolve us so far, and he provided a teaching that would allow us to consciously participate in our own evolution, which is exactly what Jesus did with his teaching of spiritual rebirth. This is why Gurdjieff called his teaching "esoteric Christianity." Both teachings were individual expressions of the Way.

So the word that came to me to conceptualize the miracle of taking evolution into our own hands by consciously living the Way (what Jesus called DOING his sayings), was the word METABIOLOGICAL; because as one LIVES the Way (be it Gurdjieff's teaching, Christ's sayings, or any wisdom saying for that matter), one transforms the consciousness of his life and REALIZES his spiritual self. Meaning: you have to live the Way for the Way to save you! This is why Dr. George Sheehan said, *"In running I found my salvation."*

The simple sport of running was a *metabiological* experience. Running transformed Dr. Sheehan's consciousness and he become more whole, more completely himself; that's why he got hooked on running and had to go for a daily run, just as I did when I began to feel the miraculous *metabiological* effects of long distance running. Long distance running satisfied my voracious need to be my true self, and like Dr. Sheehan I could also say that in running I found my salvation.

I had a lot of people in my bus, then; and although they were all "me" they all had their own needs and wants and desires, which is why my inner life was so conflicted. But with Gurdjieff's teaching I created a "Work" I, which grew strong enough to create what Gurdjieff called a "magnetic center" that attracted other teachings of the Way into my life, beginning with the sayings of Jesus; and after years of "working" on myself I'm happy to say that my bus now only has one driver!

15. The Gnostic Wisdom of Life

I was born a natural gnostic, with a small g. A natural gnostic has an intuitive sense of what the Way is. And a Gnostic with a large G is someone who lives the outer path of Gnosticism in the hope of realizing inner gnosis; meaning, an inner knowledge of what the Way is. And when he does he becomes an initiate of the Way.

Gnosis comes from the Greek word, which is usually translated as "knowledge," and a Gnostic is someone who seeks salvation through knowledge. "The knowledge that the Gnostic seeks, however, is not rational knowledge," says Stephan A. Hoeller in his book *Gnosticism: A New Light on the Ancient Tradition of Inner Knowing*; "even less is it an accumulation of information. The Greek language distinguishes between theoretical knowledge and knowledge gained through direct experience. The latter is gnosis, and a person possessing or aspiring to this knowledge is a Gnostic…for gnosis involves an intuitive process that embraces both self-knowledge and knowledge of ultimate, divine realities" (p. 2). This knowledge of ultimate, divine realities is the Way.

Jesus called the Way the "kingdom of heaven," and whenever he talked about the kingdom of heaven, the kingdom of God, or the kingdom of the Father he was talking about the Way; and when his disciples asked him, "When will the kingdom come?" Jesus replied, **"It will not come by waiting for it. It will not be a matter of saying, 'Here it is,' or 'There it is.' Rather, the kingdom of the Father is spread out upon the earth, and people do not see it"** (*Gospel of Thomas*). For Jesus, the kingdom of heaven was both a higher state of consciousness, and a redemptive path to this higher state of consciousness.

But it takes a special kind of sight, or intuitive ability to see the kingdom of heaven; or, as Jesus said, one has to have "eyes to see." This is the kind of intuitive ability that Gurdjieff's teaching of "work on oneself" awakened in me; and the more I "worked" on myself, the more I awakened to the Way, until one day I could see the

Way "spread out upon the earth." But what does this mean? This is today's spiritual musing...

When I dropped out of university in my third year of philosophy studies I left because I had been cast adrift in a sea of endless theoretical knowledge and I felt a pressing urgency to get back to *terra firma* out there, in the real world; so I left the lofty mental world of philosophical thought with Gurdjieff's teaching under my arm to guide my way.

Knowing what I know now, I believe the omniscient guiding force of life gave me an inner directive to go to university when I returned from France just so I could find Gurdjieff and initiate myself into the Creative Life Stream (what Jesus called the "water of eternal life" that flows through life) that opened up the Way to me as I "worked" on myself with Gurdjieff's teaching; and the more I opened up to the Way, the more I intuited the gnostic wisdom of life, which is why I always shouted a silent eureka every time I came upon a new **wisdom saying** that spoke the Way to me; and by **wisdom saying** I mean the special kind of redemptive knowledge that has been distilled from personal experience . For example, **trust God, but don't forget to flush the toilet.**

The gnostic wisdom of life is a big mystery, and scholars have been trying to solve this mystery for a long time. The simplest definition for gnostic wisdom has always been the knowledge of the heart, which is a special kind of knowledge that addresses soul's longing for God; and if this is the case, which I firmly believe, it would follow that the greater one's longing for God the more one's need for gnostic wisdom, and I had such a voracious need for gnostic wisdom that I devoured everything I could that would satisfy my longing to find my true self—which I came to learn was the same longing for God.

I had a harrowing sexual experience in my early twenties that catapulted me into my quest for my true self, and I did everything possible to find my true self; and dropping out of university to follow the scent of the Way landed me right back into the nitty-gritty working man's world of my youth. After working in the bush camps for a few months after I dropped out of university I was strongly nudged to start my own house-painting business in my hometown, and my trade became my classroom for all the gnostic wisdom that I would need to find my true self; and I did. But this does not explain what gnostic wisdom is.

Just as C. G. Jung hesitated to go into the profoundly mystical dimensions of his life to explain the gnostic origins of his psychology of the unconscious (his personal experiences that he shared with the world posthumously in *Memories, Dreams, Reflections* and *The Red Book*), so too do I hesitate to go there; but I have no choice.

Like St. Teresa of Avila who said in her book *The Way of Perfection,* "I shall speak of nothing of which I have no experience, either in my own life or in the observations of others," so I promised myself when I left university that I would build my life upon my own experiences and not someone else's truth; and my personal experiences of the Way as I lived Gurdjieff's teaching and Christ's sayings have given me all the assurance I need to speak frankly about the gnostic wisdom of life, but it is terrifyingly metaphysical…

I found my way to my true self by connecting the relevant dots of life that opened up a window large enough for me to "see" the Way; and every time I came upon a new **wisdom saying** (in a magazine, a new book, a television program, or from one of my painting customers; whatever the source) I added it to my list of **wisdom sayings** that would help me negotiate my way through life with greater facility; and the more I lived my **wisdom sayings**, the more the Way revealed itself to me.

It was unbelievable how the Way worked, and it gave birth to my most paradoxical saying: *to find the Way you have to live the Way; but to live the Way you have to find the Way.* This was a mystery that I did not resolve as such but was fortuitously initiated into as I lived Gurdjieff's teaching; and not until I had seven past-life regressions and connected the vital missing dots did I resolve the riddle of the gnostic wisdom of life. But as I said, it is terrifyingly metaphysical.

First I connected the dot of *creative life force* with the dot of *consciousness,* and then I connected *creative life force* with the omniscient guiding force of *Divine Spirit* when it finally dawned upon me that they were one and the same; but although I always felt that *consciousness* and *Divine Spirit* were one and the same, I did not connect all three dots (***creative life force, consciousness,*** and ***Divine Spirit***) until I had my past life regression to the body of God where I experienced myself as an un-self-realized atom of God that was sent into the world to acquire self-identity, which I could only do by evolving up the ladder of life and taking in the ***creative life force*** with each new incarnation until I gave birth to my reflective self in my first primordial human lifetime as a higher primate. Once I saw that I acquired my own individual identity by taking in the ***creative life force***, I realized that ***consciousness*** had to be the un-self-realized "I" of God, and that the whole evolutionary purpose of life was to individuate the ***creative life force*** and give birth to a new "I" of God!

When I realized this terrifying knowledge, the gnostic wisdom of life finally gave up its secret to me: the "I" of God speaks the Way with every experience that we have in life, because we take in the ***consciousness*** of life with every experience we have, which is ***Divine Spirit***, which is the omniscient guiding force of life, which is the Way; but only those that have "ears" to hear can hear it. In the simplest terms possible, then; ***the gnostic wisdom of life is the Voice of God calling us home***. This is why Jesus said that the kingdom of God was everywhere—BECAUSE LIFE ITSES IS THE WAY!

16. The Wasteland of the Soul

"Well, what did you think of the movie?" I asked Penny, as we walked to our car from the Imperial Theatre in Barrie, which I had taken her to see because of the enticing review comments ("elusive," "enigmatic," "confounding," "defies understanding") that I had read of writer-director Paul Thomas Anderson's new movie *The Master*, starring Joaquin Phoenix as the tormented soul Freddie Quell, and Seymour Hoffman as the "master" Lancaster Dodd (inspired by L. Ron Hubbard, the founder of Scientology).

Penny didn't even hesitate. "I thought it was perverted and disgusting."

I should have expected that from her, but it still took me by surprise; so I waited a moment or two before responding. Just as I was about to, she asked me what I thought of it; but my mind was blank from the moment we walked out of the theater.

"I don't know what to say. I have to process it before I can form an opinion," I said; but that wasn't good enough. She wanted to know how I felt, and I told her: "It's not what I expected. To tell you the truth, I came out of that movie feeling unclean."

"Me too," Penny said; and this is the subject of today's musing…

"Life is a journey of the self," said Ascended Master St. Padre Pio; but from where to where? Paul Gauguin asked the same question, but in his own words: *where do we come from? What are we?* And, *where are we going?* This is the central mystery of life.

In his review of *The Master,* film critic and host of REEL TALK Stephen Faber asked the question: "Should art clarify, or mystify and obscure?" And then he goes on to say, "I have always been drawn to works that bring a measure of clarity to the chaos of life." So have I; and like Stephen Faber I also feel that "clarity in art does not preclude complexity." *The Master* is a complex, ambitious, and provocative story; but, ultimately, Faber concludes, it is "a muddled journey to nowhere." And I concur.

The other night I was watching a movie on TV with Penny that was so boring I can't even recall the name, but I do remember commenting to her as I desperately fought every urge in my body to flick the remote control: "This story isn't going anywhere. It needs resolution badly." That's what *The Master* lacked—resolution. This is why reviewers called it "oblique," "opaque," "elusive," "confounding," and "enigmatic."

Penny and I were the first to leave the theater when the movie ended (the only reason I stayed to the end was to see if there was going to be some kind of resolution), and while Penny went to the lady's room I sat in the lobby and observed the people that came out after us; and every last one of the fourteen adults had an expression of befuddlement on their face. I could almost hear their thoughts: *"What the hell was that all about?"*

But it was more than befuddlement that I saw; it was a look that fought back feelings of disgust. But however hard they tried to fight back this feeling, it broke through; their eyes couldn't hide their true feelings. That look puzzled me, and it wasn't until Penny asked me how I felt about the movie did I understand that they felt the same way as I did but couldn't conceptualize their feelings—hence, their expression of befuddlement.

The movie begins with Freddie Quell (Joaquin Phoenix) obscenely humping a woman made of beach sand and then masturbating into the ocean in front of his navy comrades; and it ends with him being humped by a naked real woman that he had picked up for the night, with him asking her the same kind of questions that the "master" Lancaster Dodd (Seymour Hoffman) had asked him while "processing" him for "the Cause."

"The Cause" (Scientology) is the teaching that the "master" Lancaster Dodd has created, which includes past-life regressions to determine the origin of his followers' problems, but we never learn the origin of Freddie Quell's problems, and he has a lot of unresolved issues—which, no doubt, is why he drank that foul blend of paint thinner and alcohol that he conjured up and which fried the synapses of his brain.

Was he a damaged child? Was that the reason for his dysfunctional personality? Was it post traumatic stress disorder from his service in the war? We don't know, and we aren't given much information to work with. We have to draw our own conclusions, which makes the movie "mystifying," "enigmatic," and "confounding."

And Lancaster Dodd, the other major character in the story, is no less revealing of his character. The "master" is charming, charismatic, and mesmerizing; but he's also a mystery that offers no resolution—hence the befuddled expression that I saw on the viewers as they walked out of the theater. So if there was no resolution, what was the writer-director Paul Thomas Anderson after?

In all honesty, I have no idea. I could guess, but what would be the point? All I know is that when Penny and I walked out of that movie we felt unclean.

17. The Secret Way of Life

Do we only live one life, or many lives? Or do we live only one life that has many different expressions? Christian doctrine maintains that we only live one life, and the doctrine of reincarnation maintains that we live many lives; but I've had a thought skirting around the edges of my mind for a long time now that both doctrines are true. How can this possibly be? This is today's spiritual musing...

For some reason known only to the omniscient guiding force of life I've been strongly nudged to read short stories lately, which I've been doing between my other reading (I'm doing extensive research on C. G. Jung for *The Summoning of Noman*), and because I have such a good selection of short story anthologies (I have beautiful Folio editions of English, French, and Russian short stories, and one of novellas; plus many collections of short stories by such notables as Hemingway, Fitzgerald, Joyce, and on up to Flannery O'Connor, Updike, Mavis Gallant, and Alice Munroe), I've been delving into this fascinating genre and enjoying my reading experience immensely.

I love the short story; and I especially love reading writers that have mastered this very difficult genre, like all of the above mentioned authors. The short story is a window onto life like no other genre. We are allowed a glimpse into the human condition that automatically expands our spiritual horizons; and I say "spiritual horizons" deliberately, because I've come to realize that essentially life is a spiritual experience.

By this I simply mean that we are not a mortal physical body that may or may not have an immortal soul; we are an immortal spiritual being that has a mortal physical body; ergo, every experience that we have is essentially a spiritual experience.

Of course, I can't prove this one way or the other; but my spiritual musings are not about proving what I believe. They're about exploring my relationship with life, and everything that I have experienced has led to the realization that we are in this world to grow and evolve in the consciousness of our personal identity until we realize our spiritual nature and become our intended whole, individuated self.

Jesus called this being born again, and all of his sayings have to do with how we can give birth to our spiritual self. ***"Whoever finds the interpretation of these sayings will not taste death,"*** said Jesus in the *Gospel of Thomas*. This was Gurdjieff's teaching also. And whether one sees it or not, this is what C. G. Jung's psychology of individuation is all about as well, which he had personally realized through his own individuation process.

"Just before he died," wrote Jung's close friend Laurens van der Post in *Jung and the Story of Our Time*, "he dreamt that he saw 'high up on a high place' a boulder in the full sun. Carved into it were the words, 'Take this as a sign of the wholeness you have achieved and the singleness you have become.'"

But however the path to wholeness and singleness of self is expressed, this is our fundamental purpose in life; and the short story gives us a concentrated glimpse into the individuation process of the human condition; such as Hemingway's tragic story of a compromised writer in "The Snows of Kilimanjaro," to cite one notable example.

If we are spiritual beings and our fundamental purpose in life is to grow and evolve in our individual consciousness until we realize our spiritual nature, then it follows that we only live one life which is spiritual and all of our many and diverse mortal human lives are merely expressions of our immortal spiritual life.

In Jungian terms, this would simply mean that our spiritual self individuates through the manifestation of our multiple human lifetimes; but this concept did not hit home with me until I read what Jesus had to say about reincarnation in Glenda Green's book, *Love without End, Jesus Speaks*. Jesus compared our life to a book, and each chapter expressed one lifetime; which reconciles the two seemingly divergent views held by the doctrines of Christianity and reincarnation. According to Jesus both views are correct. ***"You actually only have one life,"*** Jesus tells Glenda. ***"It's just a very long one with many chapters."***

With poetic genius John Keats captured man's essential purpose in life and gives logic to the Way that is implicit to life. In the letter to his brother "The Vale of Soul Making" he says: "There may be intelligences or sparks of divinity in millions, but they are not Souls until they acquire identities, till each one is personally itself. Intelligences are atoms of perception—they know and they see and they are pure; in short, they are God. How then are Souls to be made? How then are these sparks which are God to have identity given them—so as even to possess a bliss peculiar to each one by individual existence? How but by the medium of a world like this?" (*Values*, by J. G. Bennett, p. 12)

Keats likened this world to a school that teaches us to grow and evolve in our own individual identity, which is essentially what the doctrine of karma and reincarnation teaches; and not until we realize our spiritual nature will we graduate from the school of life. This is what Jesus came into the world to teach us.

Unfortunately life can only teach us so much. Gurdjieff, whose teaching awakened me to the Way, said that nature (the school of life) will only evolve us so far and no further; and to realize our spiritual destiny we have to take evolution into our own hands. His teaching of "work on oneself" taught me how to do this by transforming my consciousness; as did Christ's teaching of salvation. By "doing" his sayings, one transforms his consciousness and builds his house upon a rock—meaning, one will realize wholeness and singleness of self; and only then can one graduate from the school of life.

But why can life only evolve us so far and no further? Why cannot we realize our spiritual destiny of wholeness and singleness of self in the school of life? This mystery has preoccupied man since the dawn of reason, but the answer has always been there for us to see; if we but had eyes to see, that is.

Jesus said that his teaching was only for those who had eyes to see; but he also said, ***"I am the way, the truth, and the life; no man cometh unto the Father but by me."*** Which implies a secret component to Christ's teaching that only some people can see. This is why he gave the secret teaching to his disciples and spoke to the public in parables.

"Because it is given unto you to know the mysteries of the kingdom of heaven," said Jesus to his disciples, ***"but to them it is not given. For whosoever hath, to him shall be given, and he shall have***

more abundance; but whosoever hath not, from him shall be taken away even that he hath" (Math.13: 11-12).

This begs the questions: what did his disciples have that made them ready for Christ's teaching? Why could they see the secret component of his teaching? Why could they hear the Word behind the words of his cryptic sayings and not the public?

Because life made them ready, that's why. But this only makes sense in light of the doctrine of karma and reincarnation, because it is inconceivable that one can evolve enough in one lifetime to become aware of ***the secret way*** implicit to life. This is why Paul Twitchell said that we will just keep coming back until we get it right; and getting it right simply means that we are ready to take evolution into our own hands and realize the wholeness and singleness of self that we are all spiritually destined to realize.

One person who got it right was C. G. Jung. He was evolved enough to hear the Way as it spoke to him through his patients when he underwent his "years of apprenticeship" in the Bergholzli Psychiatric Hospital in Zurich. In his commentary to Richard Wilhelm's *The Secret of the Golden Flower*, Jung wrote: "…when I began my life-work in the practice of psychiatry and psychotherapy, I was completely ignorant of Chinese philosophy, and only later did my professional experience show me that in my techniques I had been unconsciously led along ***the secret way*** which has been the preoccupation of the best minds of the East for centuries" (p. 86).

This ***secret way of life*** was the Tao, which in the West is known as the Way; and in Jung's patient efforts to listen to his mental patients in order to understand what had brought them to that condition he began to "hear" his patients personal story and discern ("see") that their story had been interrupted by life (tragedy, personal failure, heartbreak, or whatever unfortunate life circumstance), and if he could help them unblock this interruption they would reconnect with their story and continue the individuation process which would eventually make them ready to take evolution into their own hands so they could realize their wholeness and singleness of self.

This is how the school of life made Jung ready for the Way, and which he was initiated into when he had his "confrontation with the unconscious" that he recorded in *The Red Book*. So despite the fact that we cannot graduate from the school of life until we take evolution into our own hands, the natural process of karma and reincarnation will teach us everything we need to know until we are conscious enough to take karmic responsibility for our own life and realize our spiritual destiny.

And this is why I love the short story. The short story freeze-frames the unfolding story of our life and allows us to see the individuation process in all of its many fascinating manifestations. It does not tell us what *the secret way of life* is, but by freeze-framing the story of our life it allows us a concentrated glimpse of the individuation process; and after many years of reading short stories I've come to the realization that like Jung, the writer is "unconsciously led along *the secret way*" by the creative process, and not until his "apprenticeship" has evolved him enough will he awaken to *the secret way of life*.

My literary mentor Ernest Hemingway, who wrote some of the world's best short stories, never woke up to *the secret way of life* because his personal story kept getting interrupted by his uncheckable egoic needs (alcohol, sex, big game hunting, deep sea fishing, and a voracious hunger for literary fame); but the genius of his creative unconscious symbolized *the secret way of life* in the frozen carcass of a leopard that was found high up near the summit of Mount Kilimanjaro, also known as the "House of God," in the tragic story of a spent writer who had betrayed his talent in "The Snows of Kilimanjaro."

Indeed, when all is said and done our own life is *the secret way*, which is why Jesus said that the kingdom of heaven was within; but waking up to *the secret way* of our own life is what makes for the best stories in the world—like Jung's private journal that tells the story of his spiritual awakening. *The Red Book* expands the parameters of human consciousness and sets the world free from the fixed doctrines of Christianity and reincarnation; which is why Jung refused to publish it in his lifetime. The world wasn't ready to hear about *the secret way of life* then; but it is today, or my Muse wouldn't have brought it to my attention.

18. The Gurdjieff Fallacy

When I brought my book *The Summoning of Noman* to closure yesterday I began to sense the foreshadowing of what I have come to call the PCBs (post-creative blues); and not unlike the furies that haunted my classical Greek namesake Orestes, the pesky little demons were just waiting to drag me down into that netherworld of post-creative depression that every writer falls victim to whenever they finish writing a new book.

I hate the post-creative blues. Every time I fall prey to those pesky little demons I have to summon whatever courage I have left from writing my book (it takes every ounce of one's courage to write a new book) and hope that it will be enough to keep them at bay; but that never works. The PCBs always get me.

By eight o'clock last night they got me. I didn't have the strength to fight them off, so I crashed on the couch to watch TV. But it didn't matter what channel I flicked to, they all bored me. I tried reading the Saturday paper, but reading was fatiguing; so I booted my computer to see if I could ward them off by watching one of my favorite videos, John Freeman's BBC interview with Carl Jung; but as much as I loved Jung in that interview (his venerable octogenarian presence always evoked powerful emotional memories of my dream with him when he came to talk to me about my book *The Way of Soul*, and my heart always welled up with a deep, abiding love for the man and his work), it could not snap me out of the onset of my post-creative depression, so I shut down my computer and took a sleeping pill hoping that I would at least get a good night's rest.

I didn't. I slept fitfully and woke up groggy, with some vague memories of dreams; and I booted my computer, put on coffee for Penny and a pot of tea for myself, and as the water boiled for my tea I picked up Ouspenky's short novel *Strange Life of Ivan Osokin*, which I had started to read again because Ouspenky, a student of Gurdjieff and brilliant mathematician who seriously pondered the idea of eternal recurrence, brought his character Ivan Osokin back to his youth to relive twelve years of his life. This fascinated me, because *The Summoning of Noman* was the true story of my parallel life in which I was reborn into my same life and made a dramatic decision that changed the course of my life—*hence, the true story of my parallel life;* but the PCBs had me in their grip, and I couldn't read more than a page of *Strange Life of Ivan Osokin,* so I got my tea and went to my writing den.

"Maybe I'll do a spiritual musing," I mused out loud. *"I can tap into the creative life force and drive away the PCBs!"*

I had to reread some of my Gurdjieff books for *The Summoning of Noman,* and from the distance of many years my perspective on Gurdjieff's world view was not what it was when I passionately "worked" on myself with his teaching, which gave me the objectivity to see the *Gurdjieff fallacy* with so much dispassion that I decided to do a spiritual musing on it; so I called upon my Muse to explore the basic tenet of Gurdjieff's teaching, which will be the theme of today's spiritual musing…

Gurdjieff believed that not everyone is born with an immortal soul. Only some people are born with an embryonic soul which they created out of extraordinary life circumstances; and it was Gurdjieff's contention that with his teaching one could create their own soul. This is the *Gurdjieff fallacy* that persists to this day.

To make sense of what I mean by the *Gurdjieff fallacy,* let me compare it with the *Christian fallacy* that our immortal soul is created at the moment of human conception, that we only love one lifetime, and that Jesus died on the cross to atone for our sins and save us from eternal damnation. According to the *Christian fallacy,* Jesus is "the way, the truth, and the life," and ONLY through Jesus Christ can we enter the kingdom of heaven.

According to the *Gurdjieff fallacy,* we are only born with the potential to create our own soul, and if we don't realize our potential when we die we will go back to nature and become fertilizer for the life process to continue growing and evolving. As the novelist Herman Hesse said to the poet and diplomat Miguel Serrano in *C. G. Jung and Herman Hesse, A Record of Two Friendships*, "To die is to go into the Collective Unconscious, to lose oneself in order to be transformed into form, pure form." This is basic Buddhism.

STUPIDITY IS NOT A GIFT OF GOD

Gurdjieff used the analogy of an oak tree to explain to a young Fritz Peters (*Boyhood with Gurdjieff*) how nature works. Out of the thousands of acorns that an oak tree produces, maybe one might take root and grow; in like manner, out of thousands of human beings, maybe one person might take root and grow their own soul. This is the *Gurdjieff fallacy*.

In the Christian world view one can save his immoral soul from damnation by embracing Jesus Christ as their savior; and in Gurdjieff's world view one can create his own soul with the right knowledge, which Gurdjieff's teaching provides.

I was born into the Christian world view. I grew up Roman Catholic, but I left the Church at an early age to become a seeker. I tell my story in *The Summoning of Noman*. In my quest for the path to my true self, I found Gurdjieff's teaching and put it to practice. I learned how to "work" on myself with his teaching, and I did "create" my own soul.

Gurdjieff called his teaching "esoteric Christianity," because he drew from the same well of secret knowledge that Jesus did—the Essene teachings, which Jesus studied. If this is true, then both Jesus and Gurdjieff taught the same secret teaching of spiritual rebirth.

Jesus said in the *Gospel of Thomas,* **"Whoever finds the interpretation of these sayings will not taste death."** And when his disciples asked Jesus why he spoke his teaching to the public in parables but to them he spoke his teaching in secret, Jesus replied that to them it was given to know the mysteries of the kingdom of heaven, but to the public it was not given; and Jesus sums up by saying, **"Many are called but few are chosen."**

Kathleen Speeth, a student of Gurdjieff's teaching, met Gurdjieff when she was a very young girl. She was so attracted by Gurdjieff's magnetism that she went up to him and kissed him on the cheek. Gurdjieff turned to Jeanne de Salzmann, who belonged to Gurdjieff's inner circle, and said, "She has possibilities." Kathleen Riordan Speeth now teaches Gurdjieff's teaching and wrote *The Gurdjieff Work,* thus perpetuating the *Gurdjieff fallacy* that we have to create our own soul just as Christians perpetuates the *Christian fallacy* that only through Jesus Christ can we be saved; but how can I be certain that the Christian world view and Gurdjieff's world view are fundamentally flawed?

Gurdjieff said that there is only self-initiation into the mysteries of life, and Jesus said that only by *doing* his sayings could we have eternal life. As I *lived* Gurdjieff's teaching of "work on oneself" and *lived* the sayings of Jesus, I gave birth to my spiritual self one day in my mother's kitchen while she was kneading bread dough on the kitchen table. I relate this story in *The Summoning of Noman,* so I know that Gurdjieff's system works, as do the sayings of Jesus; but if they work, where's the fallacy of their teachings?

This is very complex and difficult to explain in one musing. This is why I wrote *The Summoning of Noman;* but the short answer is this: I initiated myself into the impenetrable mystery of the Divine Plan of God, which revealed to me that we are all atoms of God that are sent into these lower worlds to grow and evolve through life until we give birth to a reflective self-consciousness that continues to grow and evolve in its own individuality through the natural process of karma and reincarnation until we are ready to take evolution into our own hands and realize the full potential of our divine nature, which is what Gurdjieff's and Christ's teaching are intended to do.

This automatically begs the question: how could Gurdjieff, that remarkable man whose soul-quenching wisdom and profoundly esoteric knowledge of life was so luminous that he attracted professionals from all walks of life to his teaching—including brilliant writers and scientists—be so wrong about the essential spiritual nature of man?

But if we are not all born with an immortal soul, why is it that everyone that is regressed to a past life automatically goes back to a past life? Surely, according to Gurdjieff's world view, at least one person who was regressed to a past life would have come up blank; but in the mounting history of past-life regression therapy, this has never happened—and there is a lot of documented evidence to prove this. Many, many therapists today use past-life regression therapy in their practice, Dr. Brian L. Weiss (*Many Lives, Many Masters)*, Doctor Michael Newton (*Journey of Souls*), and Dolores Cannon (*They Walked with Jesus*) to name only three high profile past-life regression therapists. If not everyone is born with an immortal soul, how come these regressionists never hit a blank wall when they regressed their clients? All their clients were regressed to a past life.

How could this be if they did not have an immortal soul that reincarnates?

And yet the *Gurdjieff fallacy* persists. And so does the *Christian fallacy*. Why is this? Do adherents of these teachings refuse to acknowledge the unfolding spiritual consciousness of the times? The consciousness of the world has opened up to Soul's purpose in life, which is to expand the consciousness of God through the evolution of the atoms of God, and I think it is time to rethink Gurdjieff's world view as well as Christianity's.

The irony of course is that Gurdjieff's teaching works insomuch that if lived it will precipitate one's spiritual growth and one will become aware of his immortal nature, as I did; but the basic tenet of Gurdjieff's teaching is flawed, because we are all born immortal souls whose destiny is to evolve through life until we realize our potential and become spiritually self-realized, God-conscious souls. And so does Christ's teaching accomplish the same goal if one lives his sayings as he admonished. In effect, then; both teachings teach us to take evolution into our own hands so we can complete our spiritual purpose in life.

If my initiation into the Divine Plan of God is genuine, and we are all sparks of divine consciousness sent into these lower worlds to expand the consciousness of God by evolving through life to create a new "I" of God, then how did Gurdjieff and Christianity, the religion born of Jesus Christ's life and teaching, get it so wrong? And if they did get it so wrong, why do the *Gurdjieff* and *Christian fallacies* persist?

I have only one answer for this quirk in man's psyche. We are all attracted to the teaching that we need in our journey through life; but when we outgrow that teaching most of us don't have the courage to drop it and move on to another teaching that will help us complete our journey to wholeness. As the Sufis are fond of saying, "You have to die before dying." In short, we have to die to what we are not in order to realize what we are—which is Soul, the Consciousness of God. But the Divine Plan of God is merciful, because if we don't get it right in this lifetime we will just keep coming back until we do.

19. The Process of Life

I believe Gurdjieff when he said that cultures come and go but man basically remains the same; and it is to the sameness of man's nature that Gurdjieff addressed himself. "Man is asleep," said Gurdjieff; and he devoted his life to waking man up from the sleep of life; and although his teaching of self-transformation does wake man up, the paradigm that he framed it in, as comprehensive and profoundly revealing of man's nature as it may be, has made it very difficult to see the big picture of the Divine Plan of God, which is why I was strongly nudged to write a spiritual musing on *the process of life*.

I didn't want to, because it was enough for me to write a spiritual musing on the *Gurdjieff fallacy*; but my Muse persisted.

Still, I resisted.

"Why?" I asked myself. But I knew that I would only get my answer by abandoning to the creative process which has a mind of its own. I knew what had to be said, but I had no idea how my Muse would work out my thoughts to correct the perspective of Gurdjieff's teaching; and it was one thing to know what had to be said, but quite another to put it out there for the whole world to read. It gave me pause for thought.

And then I remembered the vow I made when I left university where I had gone to find answers to the two questions of my life: *who am I?* And *why am I?* I vowed that I would build my life upon the truth of my own experiences and not anyone else's; and as much as I appreciated Gurdjieff's truth, it too left me wanting. That's why I had to drop Gurdjieff's teaching and move on to another path to complete my journey through life.

That was thirty-five years ago. But while working on *The Summoning of Noman, The True Story of My Parallel Life*, I reread many of my Gurdjieff books and did extensive reading on C. G. Jung and his psychology of individuation, and what was forced upon me was the realization of my own truth that offered a glimpse of the

Divine Plan of God that put Gurdjieff's and C. G. Jung's teachings into proper perspective.

All paths are valid, and all paths lead back home to God—which is a metaphor for realizing one's spiritual self; but for a path to realize one's divine nature it has to awaken one to the Way; and the Way just *Is*. Which means that the Way is life itself; and unless one's path awakens one to the simple realization that *the process of life* is the way to realize one's essential spiritual nature, one will be forced by his own karma to come back and try again. We have no choice, because this is how *the process of life* works...

Aside from surviving open heart surgery four years ago (they didn't know if they could operate because I had heart damage from two heart attacks), which I remember observing from outside my body, I had three more amazing experiences: 1, I dreamt of rewriting the ending to *A Beautiful Mind,* the brilliant mathematician John Nash's story; 2, in another dream I saw myself being chased by Gestapo-like soldiers from one century to the next, always fleeing them in fear but never getting caught; and 3, while awake the day after surgery I saw the march of history in front of my eyes like watching a movie, from the earliest days of mankind to the modern age. This experience lasted for several hours.

I wrote a novel on my open heart surgery experience called *The Sweet Breath of Life,* and I figured out what these experiences meant. My OBE confirmed that we are more than our physical body; we are spiritual beings that inhabit a physical body. I didn't need confirmation for this, but it was nice to experience my OBE. My dream of being chased by soldiers throughout history spoke to my karma chasing after me from one life to the next; or, more precisely, it spoke to my running away from my own karma. And watching the march of history on the screen of life in front of my eyes spoke to what Gurdjieff referred to when he said that cultures change from one epoch to the next, but man basically remains the same; and altogether my three remarkable experiences spoke to *the process of life*.

When Penny and I moved to Georgian Bay eight years ago I had seven past-life regressions that gave me the missing pieces to the puzzle of life, and I pieced together the Divine Plan of God which informs us that we come into the world as un-self-realized atoms of

God that evolve through life in three stages which I discerned to be the exoteric, mesoteric, and esoteric stages of evolution.

The purpose of evolution is for the atoms of God to acquire their own individual identity—or, as dramatic as it may sound but no less true, to give birth to a new "I" of God. Once we give birth to our reflective self-consciousness in the exoteric first stage we will continue to evolve through the natural process of karma and reincarnation until we have evolved enough to take evolution into our own hands in the mesoteric second stage, which will make us ready to complete the individuation process to total self-realization consciousness in the final esoteric third stage of evolution.

This is what the ancient alchemists meant when they said that man must complete what nature left unfinished; but we cannot do this without help. This is where teachers like Jesus, Gurdjieff, and C. G. Jung come into the picture; they help us to take evolution into our own hands by teaching us how to become responsible for our own life—another way of saying that we have to stop running away and own up to the karma that has been chasing us throughout the ages; but, as Jung said to Miguel Serrano, "The path is very hard."

It has been almost forty years since I moved on from Gurdjieff's teaching; so when I was strongly nudged to revisit the Gurdjieff Work while writing *The Summoning of Noman* I reread many of my Gurdjieff books to put Gurdjieff's teaching into its proper perspective in my understanding of the Way.

The same with C. G. Jung. I reread all of my Jung books and ordered many more from Amazon, including Jung's private journal *The Red Book*, because I had a creative impulse to fit Jung's psychology of individuation into my perspective on the Way; and when I brought *The Summoning of Noman* to closure I finally understood what my Muse wanted me to realize—that as comprehensive as Gurdjieff's and Jung's teachings were, they refracted the light of the Way according to the prism of their own individuality, and the essential purpose of their teachings was to get us to live our own life. "Thank God I'm Jung and not a Jungian," said Jung, to make his point about how difficult it is to live our own life. Having said this, I can now explain what I mean by ***the process of life***...

STUPIDITY IS NOT A GIFT OF GOD

What did the alchemists (and the Gnostics as well, because they too taught the same secret teaching of the mystical union of our lower and higher self) mean when they said that we have to complete what nature left unfinished?

Nature will only evolve us so far and no further, said Gurdjieff; but he never really explained why nature could not complete man's evolution. I had to figure this out on my own, which I did when I pieced together the Divine Plan of God; and the answer has to do with the dual consciousness of man—our inner and outer self.

Soul is our inner, spiritual self. We come into the world as atoms of God, or un-self-realized Soul seeds if you will; and we evolve through life to acquire an individual identity. As we evolve from one species to the next we constellate the life force, which is the consciousness of God, until we achieve critical mass in one of the higher species and the un-self-realized soul of God becomes aware of itself as a new reflective self, as I experienced in my past-life regression to my first primordial human lifetime when I gave birth to a new "I" of God—i.e., my own reflective self-consciousness.

Once Soul has given birth to a new "I" of God the new Soul self exercise a will of its own, and by exercising self-will the self creates personal karma; and out of personal karma is born our human personality. This means that our Soul self grows in self-realization consciousness through the life force that we take in and individuate with each new personality that we create every time we reincarnate into the life process.

Our Soul self is the individuated consciousness of all our past life personalities, and our personalities are responsible for the karma that we create; which means that our Soul self is bound to the natural life process of creating and resolving karma until we evolve enough to become aware that the choices we make have karmic consequences.

This is why nature cannot evolve us to our full potential; because nature is bound by the spiritual laws of karma and reincarnation, and to evolve to our full potential we have to take evolution into our own hands by becoming responsible for our own karma.

This is easier said than done, though; which is why Jesus said, **"Many are called but few are chosen."** Jesus gave his teaching of spiritual rebirth to the world, but only those souls that had been made ready by life were attracted to Christ's teaching. And if one wasn't' ready it didn't mean that they went back into nature to become "fertilizer," as Gurdjieff believed; their physical body went back into nature to be recycled, but their Soul self went to the other side only to return to life to grow and evolve until they were ready to take evolution into their own hands, as I had to do.

I was an Essene during the time of Jesus, and I lived the same secret teaching that Jesus taught; but I didn't realize my Soul self in that lifetime. I had to return to try again, and again, and again—for such is **the process of life**.

20. The Fear of Self-knowledge

"Most people confuse 'self-knowledge' with knowledge of their conscious personalities. Anyone who has any ego-consciousness at all takes it for granted that he knows himself. But the ego knows only its own content, not the unconscious and its contents," wrote C. G. Jung in *The Undiscovered Self*; and the reason we suffer this dearth of self-knowledge is because we are afraid to know ourselves.

But why would we be afraid to know ourselves? We all have a natural curiosity about people's lives. We all want to know about the private life of our favorite movie stars; or, in my case, the private life of writers. That's why I enjoy author memoirs and biographies; so what is it about ourselves that we don't want to know?

When I wrote *Healing with Padre Pio* I went online to research his life, and then I read ten books on his life, plus the award winning biography *Padre Pio, Miracles and Politics in a Secular Age* by Sergio Luzzatto that was published after I wrote *Healing with Padre Pio;* but I had to read it because I was curious to know everything I could about the man who suffered the stigmata for fifty years and was credited with so many miracles.

I wanted to know the story of Padre Pio's life, because if I knew his story I would know his secret. Every person has their story, and every story is one's unique relationship with God—whether one believes in God or not; and to know a person's story is to know their secret. This is why we write novels—to ferret out the secret of our characters lives. So when I went into my spiritual healing sessions with the woman who channeled St. Padre Pio for my novel *Healing with Padre Pio* I had a golden opportunity to see if I had ferreted out Padre Pio's secret from all the books I had read on his life; and I believe I did: his secret was his desire to know his true self through his lord and savior Jesus Christ.

But that didn't surprise me; because I had found my true self and knew that this desire to know our true self was fundamental to human nature. I had learned from my past-life regressions that we all come from God as un-self-realized atoms, so we are all encoded with

God's DNA; and our purpose in life is to evolve in self-realization consciousness until we become aware of our divine nature. Which means that **our need to know who we are is our reason for being.** In a word, we are all driven to know who we are; and yet we are afraid to know who we are. But why the paradox? This is today's spiritual musing...

    I discovered my literary mentor in high school, and I wanted to know everything I could about Ernest Hemingway's life; and the more I learned about him over the years, the less respect I had for him as a man and husband and father. But I never lost my love and admiration for him as a writer; so, what was his secret?

    It took a long time for me to realize that if you really want to know about the private life of a writer you have to read their fiction, because writers write fiction to get to the truth of who and what they are (whether intentionally or unintentionally); and the story that revealed Hemingway's secret was "The Snows of Kilimanjaro."

    This story opens with a paragraph about Mt. Kilimanjaro, the highest mountain in Africa, which is also called the "House of God." There is the frozen carcass of a leopard near the summit, but no one knows why it is there; and the story goes on to reveal the private hell of a writer's life that is dying of gangrene on a safari.

    A thorn scratched Harry's knee when he was trying to get a picture of a water-buck, and failing to put iodine on the scratch it became septic; so Harry is dying of gangrene while waiting for the plane to take him to a hospital. As he waits for the plane he reminisces about his life. In these painful reminiscences Hemingway is at his most autobiographical and reveals the dark secret of his unfulfilled life—*self-betrayal*.

    Harry compromised his talent for the financial security that he got from the wealthy women he married; and everything that I read about Hemingway's life (my favorite book being *Papa Hemingway*, a personal memoir by A. E. Hotchner) shed light on "The Snows of Kilimanjaro" and spoke to the truth that Hemingway feared to accept about his own life. Hemingway could write about his life truthfully in his fiction, always beginning every story with "one true sentence" as he tells us in his memoir *A Moveable Feast*; but he could not be truthful to himself about his compromised life; that's why his third wife and journalist Martha Gellhorn called him a "pathological liar."

For years scholars have been trying to figure out why Hemingway would include the information about the frozen carcass of a leopard near the summit of the "House of God," but it wouldn't be a stretch to say that the leopard symbolizes man's natural desire to go back home to God; and because no one knows what it was doing so high up the mountain speaks to man's lack of self-knowledge. This is what attracted me to C. G. Jung.

"My soul, my soul, where are you?" writes Jung in *The Red Book*. "At that time, in the fortieth year of my life, I had achieved everything that I had wished for myself. I had achieved honor, power, wealth, knowledge, and every human happiness. Then my desire for the increase of these trappings ceased, the desire ebbed from me, and horror came over me" (*The Red Book*, A Reader's Edition, p. 127).

When Jung awakened to the shocking truth that the Faustian price he paid for his success was his own soul, he went into the depths of his unconscious to look for it and he records his astonishing journey in *The Red Book*; and although I had long sensed Jung's secret as the subtext of all his writing, it wasn't until his family gave permission to have *The Red Book* published fifty years after his death that Jung revealed the secret of his relationship with God—the same secret that I had ferreted out of life in my own quest for my lost soul: **"This life is the way, the long sought-after way to the unfathomable, which we call divine. There is no other way. All other ways are false."**

I had come to the same realization that life is the Way; but realizing that life is the Way and living the Way is what separates the men from the boys, because it takes courage to accept the shocking truth that our own life is the way to satisfy our deepest desire to be who we are meant to be. Hemingway couldn't do it and took his own life because he could not live with the truth of what he had become; but Jung did.

A few days before his death Jung told of a dream he had, the last one he was able to communicate. He saw a great round stone in a high place and on it was engraved: "And this shall be a sign unto you of Wholeness and Oneness." Jung reclaimed his lost soul, and out of his journey, which he called his "confrontation with the unconscious," he built his own psychology of individuation—a gnostic elucidation of the path to one's true self.

Jung and I had a meeting of minds. This is why he came to me in a dream one night to talk about my book *The Way of Soul* which was not published yet. Over there, on the other side, it was published; and Jung wanted to talk about "the alpha and omega of the self" because he wanted to know the secret of my life.

I wrote a novel called *The Waking Dream* with Jung as a central character; and the premise of my novel was **the secret way of life**, which Jung called the "individuation process" and I called the "Way of Soul." But whatever we call it, it is the same shocking truth that the only way to realize our longing for wholeness is by being true to ourselves.

This is why we're terrified of self-knowledge. We don't want to accept the moral obligation that comes with the realization that only we can save ourselves. As Gurdjieff said, nature will only evolve us so far; and to satisfy our inherent longing for wholeness we have to take responsibility for our own evolution, and this few people want to do.

PART THREE

"I think stupidity is original sin, and I think we've all got it."

Martha Gellhorn,
Hemingway's Third Wife
THE OUTSIDERS INTERVIEW
John Pilger

21. Good Lives Well Lived Are Heroic

I was watching an interview of the Canadian writer Wayson Choy on a program called *Distinguished Artists* last week (this was the second time I saw it), and although I heard **the language of life** speaking to me in something that Wayson Choy said, and which I took note of because I wanted to explore it in a spiritual musing, I never got around to it; but this morning while waiting for my tea to steep I was reading a book review of James Salter's new novel, *All That Is* (he was eighty-seven when he produced this novel, and the review in *Harper's* April 2013 is titled "The autumnal works of James Salter") and it triggered my memory of Choy's comment about a vein of literary gold that has not been satisfactorily mined by creative writers. What Choy said was highlighted for me again in my mind by the golden light of the Way, and which I took note of again because once more I was nudged to explore it in a spiritual musing: "**Good lives well lived are heroic.**" I knew this to be true; but why? This is today's spiritual musing...

It costs to be a good person. I remember a line that James Rockford used in the TV drama *The Rockford Files*, in reference to his time spent in prison, "No good deed goes unpunished." That sounds almost sacrilegious; but it's true, because the virtue of goodness threatens the status quo, and the status quo wields power in prison as it does in life.

The status quo is the existing state of affairs; and the existing state of affairs always runs the show, as the expression goes. This is why politicians lead by polls. Whichever way the wind blows, that's where they will lead to stay in power. Ironic, but true.

There's a real mystery here that I have to explore; so I'm going to step aside and let my Muse speak; and by Muse I mean my creative unconscious. That's the only way I can get to the bottom of this...

Why would Socrates make goodness the most noble of all the virtues? Socrates taught the secret teaching of the Way, which he couched in his philosophy. The secret teaching of the Way is the path to one's true self. One's true self is Soul, which is trapped in the little self of one's personality; and the only way out of one's self-created prison is to transform one's consciousness, which Socrates said we can do by living a life of virtue.

"And what is purification but the separation of the soul from the body (the consciousness of our little self), *as I was saying before; the habit of the soul gathering and collecting herself into herself, out of all the courses of the body; the dwelling in her own place alone, as in another life, so also in this, as far as she can; the release of the soul from the chains of the body,"* said Socrates in Plato's *Phaedo*. And Socrates illustrates Soul's prison with his now famous allegory of the cave in Book VII of Plato's *Republic*.

Socrates doesn't expressly spell it out, but one gathers and collects Soul into herself by living a life of virtue, of which goodness is the most effective. I know this to be true, because I made the virtue of goodness central to my path to my true self.

I went out of my way to practice the virtue of goodness, like doing volunteer work for Habitat for Humanity every summer for seven years; picking up hitchhikers and giving them meal money every time I drove to Thunder Bay for supplies and the north shore communities for work; picking wild blueberries for some of my senior painting customers, cutting my neighbor's lawn, and on and on. That's how I learned what Jesus meant by storing our treasures in heaven. Goodness is the energy that we need to transform the consciousness of our little self so we can escape from the prison of our own consciousness; and my goal, as I've just written about in *The Summoning of Noman,* was to escape from the prison of my own consciousness.

The virtue of goodness speaks to self-sacrifice; and the self that we sacrifice is our own little self—which is why Socrates said, *"the true disciple of philosophy is ever pursuing death and dying,"* and Jesus said, **"he that loseth his life shall find it."**

Our little self is our ego-personality, and ego is by nature selfish and does not want to be sacrificed. It has taken nature millions of years to evolve our individual self, which is made up of the consciousness of *being* and *becoming*; but to *be*, our ego-personality has to *become*; and to *become* one has to struggle with life. This is how we evolve in self-realization consciousness. As Paul Twitchell said, "All the growth is in the hassle."

But survival makes us selfish. This is why it's so hard to do good. When one does good he is giving of himself, and ego does not want to be sacrificed. This is why Jesus said that when we do good we must be secretive. ***"But when thou doest alms, let not thy left hand know what the right hand doeth; that thine alms may be in secret. And thy Father which seeth in secret himself shall reward thee openly"*** (Math. 6:3-4). The virtue of goodness transforms our ego-personality by teaching us to not be selfish. In the words of Socrates, we gather and collect Soul into herself. This is how we become our true self simply by doing good; but why should this threaten the status quo?

As preposterous as it may sound, it's because society can only tolerate a certain level of goodness in people. Too much goodness makes people uneasy with guilt, and people don't want to feel guilty; that's why society sarcastically refers to people that make a habit of doing good as "do-gooders." And this begs the question: why should people feel uneasy with guilt because of another person's goodness?

This speaks to the question of why we are here, which is to grow and evolve in self-realization consciousness until we become aware of our divine nature. To become aware of our divine nature we have to transform the consciousness of our selfish ego-personality, which does not want to be transformed; ergo, the reason why people feel guilty when they are reminded that they have an inherent obligation to realize their true self.

This is the root source of man's conflict with himself, which can be spelled out in the simplest terms possible as the battle between our selfish ego-personality and our inherent longing to be our true self. In a word, the only way we can be our true self is to transcend the consciousness of our ego-personality, which cannot be done through the natural process of life (karma and reincarnation) because man is by nature inherently selfish. This is our dilemma. We have an inherent spiritual imperative to realize our divine nature, and we have an inherent biological imperative to survive in life, which makes us naturally selfish; but we cannot realize our divine nature by being selfish. Thus giving rise to man's existential angst that has led many people to conclude that life is meaningless and absurd.

This is why we have to take evolution into our own hands to complete what nature cannot complete; and one way to take evolution into our own hands is to practice the virtue of goodness, because the more good we do the more we grow in our spiritual nature. And one day we will realize our divine nature, as I did that summer day in my mother's kitchen when I shifted my center of gravity from my ego-personality to my Soul self and realized my own immorality. In Christ's words, I gave birth to my spiritual self. Which brings me back to the theme of today's musing—**good lives well lived are heroic.**

But before I get back to the theme, let me risk revealing the esoteric (metaphysical) reason why people have a natural resentment for people that do good. This puzzled me for a long time. But because I experienced this natural resentment from people so often in my life I set out to solve the mystery, and all the pieces came together when I realized that the energy of the Way is inherently self-transcending; which means that the more one realizes the energy of the Way (spiritual consciousness), the more his state of consciousness will affect the consciousness of anyone who is less spiritually self-realized.

But it's in how the more spiritually self-realized affect the less spiritually self-realized that creates the dramatic tension between them. The personal energy field of the more spiritually self-realized person is more replete with the inherently self-transcending energy of the Way; which means that when the less spiritually self-realized are in the company of the more spiritually self-realized they are automatically lifted to a higher state of spiritual consciousness, which makes them more aware of their ego-personality than they care to be; hence the reason for their psychic unease and natural resentment—because their ego-personality does not want to be made aware of its selfish nature, like the woman who said to me one day *"Are you crazy?"* when I told her that all my work for St. Sylvester's Historic Mission Church in my hometown of Nipigon was voluntary. My charity offended her sense of values, and she called me "crazy" essentially for being a good person!

This realization gave birth to my saying ***you can only be so good before society turns on you.*** Which is why mystery schools practice the Law of Silence. It's to protect the initiate of the Way from the course energies of life. Jesus told his disciples to be as wise as serpents and gentle as doves, because he knew that his teaching would bother some people; which ties in very nicely with why good lives well lived are heroic.

An immigrant father who works sixteen hours a day seven days a week running his gas bar and convenience store so his children can go to university (his oldest boy wants to become a medical doctor) sacrifices his life for his children. One would not think there is heroism in this, but there is heroism in any form of self-sacrifice; and the more one sacrifices their life for the good of another, the more heroic they are.

This is why Wayson Choy, who was raised in Vancouver's Chinatown by both his adoptive parents and his extended community which he reflects in his novels *The Jade Peony* and *All That Matters*, said that there is a vein of literary gold to be mined in the well-lived lives of good people; and by well-lived he meant ***purposive goodness*** like the hard-working father who sacrifices his life for the welfare of his children.

"What I came to understand about life," said Choy after his life-threatening illness that deepened everything for him, "is that common acts of decency are often the most meaningful ones." That's a simple example of ***purposive goodness***.

For years I blamed my parents for their paucity of ***purposive goodness***. They had their hands full just to survive with a large family in a foreign land; but not until I was mature enough to realize how difficult it was just to survive (let alone in a new country) when one has no skills other than the will to survive was I able to forgive my parents for their inability to transcend their circumstances. This is how I came to the realization that a parent's first obligation in life is to prepare their children for survival in this harsh, cruel world; and why we admire—or resent, depending upon our state of consciousness—those that do. And this is why I summed up my philosophy of life with the cheeky saying: ***the ultimate purpose of life is to simply be a good person.***

22. The Mystical Power of Story

I didn't expect it so soon, but it happened this morning: I was online doing research on professor Dr. Jacob Needleman for something he wrote that I felt would be a good entry point for the spiritual musing I was planning to write ("Life Only Makes Sense When We Know Why We Are Here"), but for some reason known only to my Muse I gravitated to a Bill Moyers interview with the acclaimed author Barry Lopez who discusses nature, spirit, and the human condition. Lopez is an essayist, author and short story writer whose books include *Arctic Dreams*, winner of the National Book Award, and *Of Wolves and Men*.

From the first two or three sentences that he uttered, I knew that Barry Lopez was a kindred spirit; and by this I mean an initiate of the Way of Soul.

The Way of Soul is the natural path to one's true self. It is the conscious path of self-individuation; which simply means that Barry Lopez had come to the realization that the path to one's true self involves the union of opposites—the good and the evil of life. Only by this mystical union can one be made whole; a truly Jungian perspective.

The more I listened, the more Lopez proved me right; and then he confirmed my intuition with something that he said about the spiritual nature of language that gave me the entry point I needed for the spiritual musing I wanted to write on the secret meaning of words; hence my spiritual musing today: the mystical power of story...

I love how the omniscient guiding force of life works. One morning last week while reading *More Matter* (a collection of John Updike's essays, book reviews, and criticism) as I waited for my herbal tea to steep the idea struck me to write a musing on words, because Updike's enormous respect for *le mot juste* and prodigious vocabulary sparked an idea for a musing on the mystical nature of words that can be traced back to St. John's Gospel: *"In the beginning was the Word, and the Word was with God, and the Word was God. The same was in the beginning with God. All things were made by him; and without him was not anything made that was made. In him was life; and the life was the light of men. And the light shineth in darkness, and the darkness comprehended it not"* (John 1: 1-5). But I had no point of entry for my musing; so I jotted the idea in my notebook, and waited.

    I then remembered an exchange of words that went on between William Faulkner and Ernest Hemingway that I thought might be a good point of entry. The story goes that in one of his drunken moments Faulkner wrote Hemingway to taunt him that he was afraid to use big words. Hemingway, whose writing vocabulary has been calculated by Hemingway scholars to be no more than nine hundred words, wrote back and said (no doubt in one of his drunken pugilistic moments): "You don't need big words to express big emotions."

    I loved Hemingway's writing, and still do; but I could never emulate him. I tried, but his style was too tight for me. I felt like I was straitjacketing my mind trying to write like him. James Joyce on the other hand gave me all the room I needed to express myself. So did John Updike's style. Too much so in fact, because Updike's style seems to stretch the boundaries of language to near transcendence; which could be why I cannot remember any of his stories. As real as they are when I am reading them, they evaporate into thin air a day or so later. Not Hemingway, though; his stories stay with you for years.

    Why is that? What makes a story memorable? Was Hemingway onto something with his comment to Faulkner? Hemingway once said that he read the Bible from cover to cover once a year; but given his reputation for lying one wonders if this was true. And yet, he copied the simple sentence structure of the Bible; that's how some Hemingway scholars think he created his lean evocative style. Personally, I think Hemingway fluked his style when he was a journalist in Paris and cabled his stories back to the Toronto Star and declared that "cablese" was a new style of writing—short and to the point sentences. But he maximized the effect of his lean style with what he called his "iceberg theory" of writing, which he put to effective use in his first novel *The Sun Also Rises* by not revealing why his protagonist Jake Barnes never made love with Lady Brett

Ashley. The answer is in the story, but it is implied; this is the emotional impact that Hemingway sought in his stories.

He got the title of his first novel from *Ecclesiastes*, so there may be something to his reading the Bible yearly; but that's neither here nor there. The point is that a writer has to find the style that reflects the man, and Hemingway was a physically-centered man. Joyce was an intellectually-centered man. Two extreme individuals, which is reflected in their extreme styles; and I try to be the best of both in my style. But whatever the style, creative writers are storytellers, and the story *is* the message. This is the mystery...

I got my first clue to the mystical power of story when I was researching G. G. Jung for my book *The Summoning of Noman*. When Jung worked at the Bergholzli Hospital in Zurich he learned from his mental patients that they had been disconnected from their life story (their karmic purpose in life), and he realized that if he could help them to reconnect they had a chance at living a normal life; and while reading *Jung and the Story of Our Time,* by Laurens van der Post, I learned that the Bushman, the first people of South Africa, passed on their stories in secret because they contained powerful messages about life that they guarded closely. Stories were the medium of their life wisdom, as it were.

"I realized that the story was their most precious possession and they were protecting it the best way they could," wrote Laurens van der Post. "They knew how dangerous it was to have a foreigner, above all a white foreigner, in on the secret of any of their stories, because they might destroy it either by making fun of it, using it against them, or merely not joining in its progression as they did" (p. 124).

The close juxtaposition of these two pieces of information (Jung's insight about one's life story garnered from his patients, and the Bushman's reverence for their stories) sparked an epiphany: stories are conveyers of the Word, which is the Light of God, which is the Way, which is the omniscient guiding force of life—ergo, stories *are* the Way!

This is the mystical power of story; but it only makes sense when one comes to terms with the *I Am* principle of the Way, which is implicit to life. This principle is the inherently reconciling power of the consciousness of God, which is Soul.

In effect, Soul is forever reconciling itself with itself by way of karma—*I Am THAT I Am.* This is the Way of Soul, the natural process of self-individuation; which means that every person's karmic destiny is the seed and essence of their personal story, and as Jung realized, when a person is disconnected from their story they stop growing because they have interrupted the natural individuation process of their karmic destiny, and only when reconnected with their karmic destiny will they continue on their journey to wholeness.

This is why we love stories; they let us in on **the secret way** of a person's life, and we feel privileged to be given such secret knowledge.

For example, Hemingway revealed Harry's secret knowledge in the short story "The Snows of Kilimanjaro." Harry interrupted the story of his life by compromising his karmic destiny (his natural talent for writing) for the financial security that he got from the wealthy women that he married. "He had destroyed his talent by not using it, by betrayals of himself and what he believed in," wrote Hemingway in "The Snows of Kilimanjaro."

Harry was dying of gangrene from a scratch that infected his leg, and he knew that he had not fulfilled his purpose in life as a writer; and the frozen carcass of the leopard near the summit of Mt. Kilimanjaro (the "House of God") symbolizes Harry's lack of self-knowledge ("No one has explained what the leopard was seeking at that altitude"), because if Harry had known what his Faustian bargain would have cost him he might not have compromised himself and realized his destined purpose as a writer. Harry was not true to himself; and he is dying unresolved as he waits for the plane to take him to the hospital.

Karmic destiny is our individual purpose in life, and as long as we are true to our karmic destiny we are living our life story; but when we detract from our karmic destiny we interrupt the story of our life and become our own worst enemy, like Harry in "The Snows of Kilimanjaro." (I've read enough Hemingway biographies to know that Hemingway was his own worst enemy, which is why he ended up taking his own life; and he did tell us that "The Snows of Kilimanjaro" was his most autobiographical story.)

The irony of course is that most of us don't know what our karmic destiny is, and we go through life wondering what our purpose is; but that's only because we haven't evolved enough yet for our karmic destiny to call us as it does some people who know from an early age what they are meant to be.

Doctors, poets, artists, politicians—many people are called by their karmic destiny; and if they do not heed the call they suffer the anxiety of not being true to their karmic destiny, which is their life story. But I explored this theme in my little book *Why Bother? The Riddle of the Good Samaritan;* so I need not expound upon it here.

Being true to our karmic destiny is our purpose in life, then. This is why when our story gets interrupted we suffer the anxiety of not being true to ourselves; but if we don't get it right in this life, we will just keep coming back until we do. Having said this let me now explore the mystical power of story…

Our karmic destiny is our personal destiny, which we create from life to life by the choices we make; so our karmic destiny is fixed only insomuch that we have to fulfill our karmic obligations to life and changeable insomuch that we are free to alter the course of our karmic destiny. This is the mystery of our life story.

In effect, we write the script of our own life story; but as every writer knows, there is a mystical component to story writing that is difficult to comprehend. As much as we are the authors of our own life story, like the writer whose story will find its own way so will our life story find its own way; and this is the mystical power of story that speaks to our inherent, pre-ordained spiritual destiny.

This is difficult to comprehend, because it is almost impossible to reconcile free choice with a fixed spiritual destiny; and the only resolution that makes any sense is the paradoxical realization that **we are free to become what we are meant to be.**

We are all meant to become spiritually self-realized, God-conscious Souls; this is our spiritual destiny that is encoded in our spiritual DNA. But because we have free will we create personal karma, which determines our karmic destiny. Our karmic destiny is our life story, and written into the script of our life story is our encoded spiritual destiny; so no matter how we write the script of our life (one person may become a poet, another a doctor, architect, school teacher, nurse—whatever; each person writes their own script), we are all pre-scripted to realize our spiritual destiny whether we like it or not.

So our purpose in life is to make sure that our karmic destiny conforms to our pre-scripted spiritual destiny; because if it doesn't we will be dragged yelling and screaming (some of us cursing God, even) until we bring our karmic destiny into agreement with our spiritual destiny.

Our life story then is our personal relationship with our pre-scripted spiritual destiny, which makes our life story unique because no two people have the same karmic destiny; which is why the wounded healer Carl Jung had so much reverence for the personal story of every one of his patients, and people in general. And this is why we love to read stories; because no two stories can ever be the same. But just what is the mystical power of story?

Throughout history story has always held our attention; and despite the fear of the novel going by way of the Dodo bird as novelist Philip Roth thinks, story will always be with us—because story *is* the Way, and the Way *is* life! *"In the beginning was the Word, and the Word was with God, and the Word was God,"* said St. John. *"In him was life; and the life was the light of men...And the light shineth in darkness, and the darkness comprehended it not."* But some of us catch a glimpse of this divine light and align our karmic destiny with our spiritual destiny.

Barry Lopez did. He is not only a storyteller; he is also a self-initiate of the **secret way of life**. And in his interview with Bill Moyers he unconsciously connected the dots of story and the Word of God, thereby revealing the mystical power of story.

Moyers remembered an account of a remark that Barry Lopez made 25, 26 years earlier when he received the National Book Award for *Arctic Dreams*; about a word that he had come across when he was visiting Japan. And Barry Lopez replied that he was with the novelist Kazumasa Hirai. "We call him a novelist," he said "But he was just a storyteller. He's like me. And I would ask him or anybody I was with, 'What do you mean when you say you're a storyteller? What do you do?' Because I wanted to know what I'm listening for...I'm not interested in structure of sentences. What I want to know is how do you know how to behave? How do you know what to do as a person for other people? How do you know? What do you do?"

"As a storyteller?" Moyers asked.

"Right," Lopez answered. "As a storyteller. And Kazumasa San said to me, 'Your work is to take care of the spiritual interior of language.' And he said in Japanese this word we use, kotodama, which means that each word has within it a spiritual interior. The word is like a vessel that carries something ineffable (*the Word is the Soul of life, which is the Way*). And you must be the caretaker for that. You must be careful when you use language to look at every part of the word and make sure that you're showing respect for it in the place that you've given it to live in the sentence. But I see all of us engaged in the same thing," Lopez explains to Bill Moyers. "And that is the invention of the story. And the story to me is the brilliance of storytelling…it's the best protection we have against forgetting (*our life story*)…And I'm so glad to be reminded (*by storytellers*) of what I intend to do and who I am—and how I want to conduct myself in the world."

This is the core message of story (myths, novels, short stories, plays, and poetry)—**to remind us to be true to own life story.**

What Barry Lopez is talking about is the Way, because **story *is* the Way,** the path to our true self; and the storyteller is a messenger of the Way, whether he knows it or not—because with every story that he tells he reveals the ***secret way of life.***

This is the mystical power of story!

23. 10,000 Hours, Past Lives, Or Luck of the Draw?

My titles come to me. Seldom do I get an idea for writing without a title. In fact, my idea *is* the title; and the other night shortly after I got into bed the title for a spiritual musing came to me and I had to go to my writing den to jot it down in my ideas/quotes/musings notebook: "10, 000 Hours, Past Lives, or Luck of the Draw?"

The idea for this spiritual musing was set free from the depths of my creative unconscious by something that Malcolm Gladwell wrote. I thought it was in his book *What the Dog Saw,* which I had sitting in one of the piles of books on the floor of my den; so I checked it out, but it must have been his other book, *Outliers.*

I didn't have that one; but I had read several reviews when it came out, plus I had seen the author interviewed on TV and was very impressed by his idiosyncratic personality, quick humor, and self-possessed manner, and I remembered recently seeing a hardcover copy of *Outliers* at a discounted price in Coles bookstore in Midland; so the following morning being Saturday when I always drive into Midland to pick up my weekend *National Post* (I love following Conrad Black's column. He's an "Ozymandian personality" type who has been humbled by life and which he now reflects in his column, as he did in this Saturday's with his recent blindness scare, "I Can See Again"), and I checked Coles but couldn't find the discounted copy; so I asked one of the clerks if they had a copy in stock.

The lady with glasses walked me over to the designated aisle (no wonder I couldn't find it; it was categorized as History/Politics) and pointed to the four freshly printed paperback editions. It was $19.95 Canadian. I got a copy. And then I went over to the magazine rack and selected the latest *New Yorker* magazine (April 2013) because they had some articles that excited my curiosity: PROFILES, The Last Book, "Why James Salter isn't famous" (I had just read a review of Salter's novel *All That Is* in *Harper's*); LIFE & LETTERS, John le Carre's article, "Filming a novel with Richard Burton" (I never read the novel, but I saw the movie "The Spy Who Came in from the Cold"); and FICTION, a new story by one of the most scintillating writers I have ever read, "The Night of the Satellite," by T. Coraghessan Boyle (my interest in story had just been re-kindled by my last spiritual musing, "The Mystical Power of Story"); so I *had* to buy the magazine out of sheer coincidental imperative, but to my surprise when I went to the counter to pay for my items the cashier told me that the lady with glasses was checking to see if they still had a discounted copy of *Outliers* in the store.

She couldn't find it up front, so she went to the back room and came out holding the last discounted copy. It was $7.99, which was a twelve dollar saving. I thanked the lady, grateful for the considerate service, and paid for my items. I was also smiling to myself because I knew that this was proof that I had slipped into the "synchronicity zone," and by this I mean that place when one is in sync with the universe. "God's in His heaven—/All's right with the world!" said Robert Browning, expressing perfectly how I felt.

"Outliers" is defined as 1: "something that is situated away from or classed differently from a main or related body; 2: a statistical observation that is markedly different in value from the others of the sample." And Malcolm Gladwell's *Outliers* is an inspired outside-the-box look at why people achieve success in life.

The basic premise of *Outliers* is that people succeed not because of their individual talent, as such; but because of the environment, community, and culture that they were exposed to growing up. "It makes a difference where and when we grew up," writes Gladwell. "The culture we belong to and the legacies passed down by our forebears shape the patterns of our achievement in ways we cannot begin to imagine. It's not enough to ask what successful people are like, in other words. It is only by asking where they came *from* that we can unravel the logic behind who succeeds and who doesn't" (*Outliers*, p. 19).

Success, according to the meticulous research Gladwell did, is the result of what sociologists like to call "accumulative advantage," or what sociologist Robert Merton famously called the "Mathew Effect" after the New Testament verse in the Gospel of Mathew: ***"For unto everyone that hath shall be given, and he shall have abundance; but from him that hath not shall be taken away even that which he hath"*** (Math. 25: 29).

STUPIDITY IS NOT A GIFT OF GOD

Jesus is speaking about the Spiritual Law of Attraction in this verse, which simply states that **like attracts like**; or, as is commonly understood in the exoteric vernacular, "much gathers more." It's from the Spiritual Law of Attraction that we get expressions like, "nothing succeeds like success," "it takes money to make money," "the more you have, the more you get," "birds of a feather flock together," "misery loves company," "it takes one to know one," and so on; all speaking to what Robert Merton has called the "Mathew Effect" that Gladwell explores in his analysis of success in *Outliers* and from which Chapter Two, "The 10,000-Hour Rule," my beneficent Muse inspired today's spiritual musing…

When I began writing my musing this morning I knew that I was definitely in the "synchronistic zone" when my creative unconscious reminded me of something that Jesus said in Glenda Green's book *Love without End, Jesus Speaks* that not only compliments what Gladwell said about success in *Outliers*, but expands upon his theme with such esoteric clarity that it spoke directly to the title of my musing.

Outliers address the sociological factors of success—cultural legacies and luck of the draw; but it does not address the hidden, unseen dimensions of success—like past lives and the karmic power of personal destiny. My omniscient Muse however knew that there's much more to success than meets the eye; that's why I was given the title "10,000 Hours, Past Lives, or Luck of the Draw?"

Since I was familiar with the esoteric dimension of success I didn't have to research that for my musing; but I had to read Gladwell's book to see how the "Mathew Effect" applied to his theme in *Outliers*. That's why I had to buy a copy. I was also motivated to buy it because of what Jesus said in Glenda Green's book *Love without End, Jesus Speaks*: ***"The third principle of success is so integral to life that most people overlook it as a basis for achievement and fulfillment: Simply follow life and the living…As we follow life and the living, we move forward. Life is being created anew each day, and consciousness is expanding with every new burst of life*** (Chapter 13, "Pathways to Success," p. 308); and by reading Malcolm Gladwell, a feature writer for *The New Yorker* magazine, I would be following life and the living—i. e., the refreshing currents of contemporary thought.

This speaks to the power of the creative unconscious and personal story. We all have a personal, karmic destiny; and life always provides us opportunities to fulfill our personal destiny. Our personal destiny is our life story, and Gladwell explores the life story of successful people in *Outliers*—like the founder of Microsoft Bill Gates and cofounder of Apple Computer Steve Jobs; both men whose success Gladwell proves to be the result of the "accumulative effect" of the opportunities afforded them by their environment.

Gladwell connected the dots and saw that success is not a matter of individual talent, as such; but of the opportunities afforded a person to cultivate their talent (with nothing less than 10,000 hours of concerted effort in one's chosen field) in order to achieve success. But the larger paradigm that allows all the variables of success to converge in a person's life is the dynamic of karmic destiny—which can be realized or not depending upon whether one exploits the opportunities afforded him by life.

Gladwell offers a clear example in the life story of Chris Langan, a man whose IQ was one hundred and ninety-five, forty-five points higher than Einstein's one fifty, but whose childhood did not provide him with the "practical intelligence" necessary to take advantage of the opportunities that life afforded him to achieve success.

Chris Langan grew up in dire poverty. This deprived him of the "practical intelligence" and "sense of entitlement" necessary to take advantage of life's opportunities; which speaks to Gladwell's premise that where you come *from* goes a long way to determining one's success. It's not that one cannot succeed if he isn't brought up in an environment that nurtures patterns of success ("practical intelligence" and a "sense of entitlement"); it means that one has to work against the odds to succeed in life; some do, but most get swept up by the sweeping currents of life.

This suggests that successful people who were brought up in an environment that nurtured patterns of success lucked out on life; but was it the luck of the draw that Bill Gates and Steve Jobs were born into a cultural milieu that nurtured success and Chris Langan wasn't, or was it their personal karmic destiny?

STUPIDITY IS NOT A GIFT OF GOD

The only way to prove this would be to know the past-life history of a person's life story, which would not cut it in *The New Yorker* magazine where Gladwell writes feature articles like "How David Beats Goliath," the seed idea for his new book *David and Goliath*; because society is not evolved enough yet to embrace the larger paradigm of human evolution. This perspective would only be laughed at by the exoterically minded editors at *The New Yorker*. Still, to see the bigger picture of success we have to see the whole story of one's personal history, which would include their past lives.

"Karma is a choice," St. Padre Pio told me in one of my spiritual healing sessions, which I never quite fully grasped; but after reading *Outliers* I can see what he meant: we are given opportunities to succeed in life, but whether we take advantage of them depends upon the choices we make. And successful people have made choices that allowed them to exploit the opportunities offered them—whether they were offered by pure circumstance, or by the power of their karmic destiny to draw the opportunities into their life; and what Gladwell makes clear in *Outliers* is that those who took advantage of the opportunities afforded them WORKED an average of 10,000 hours to master their discipline which "catapulted" them to success—like the Beatles who played their music in German night clubs no less than ten thousand hours before they rose to "instant" stardom.

There are innumerable stories of how synchronicity played a part in one's success, as Robert H. Hopcke tells us in his book *There Are No Accidents, Synchronicity and the Stories of Our Lives*, so I need not expound upon this theme; but with respect to *Outliers,* I have to say that as informative and enlightening as Malcolm Gladwell's perspective on success is, it makes much more sense when we see it within the framework of the larger paradigm of one's karmic history—which, of course, means one's past lives.

"Our lives have a narrative structure, like that of novels," writes Robert H. Hopcke, "and at those moments we call synchronistic this structure is brought to our awareness in a way that has a significant impact upon our lives" (p. 8).

This "narrative structure" is our karmic destiny, which is the story of our life, and synchronicities are opportunities afforded us by the omniscient guiding force of life; but whether we act upon them or not is entirely our choice. This is the fundamental reason why some people succeed and others don't. It all has to do with the choices we make—*regardless of how informed they are or where we come from!*

24. Life after Life

I have known for quite some time now that the creative unconscious will pop up new seed ideas like spring flowers when the world is ready for them, so it didn't surprise me when I heard that a novel had been published about parallel lives; that's why I had to listen to Elenor Wachtel's show *Writers and Company* on CBC radio last Sunday.

Elenor's guest was the English writer Kate Atkinson, and her novel was *Life after Life*, whose heroine Ursula Todd keeps dying and dying again; the central premise being that we can change the destiny of our life by the choices we make.

In effect, every choice we make has within it the potential of a whole new destiny—just as every seed has within it the potential of its own reality; like an acorn seed has within it the potential of becoming an oak tree; a tomato seed has within it the potential of becoming a tomato plant that will produce new tomatoes, and so on. Every choice that our soul makes is its own spring flower; that's what makes Atkinson's novel so effective.

Kate Atkinson cleverly plotted out the many lives that her heroine Ursula Todd lived because her soul made different choices for the same life. This sounds confusing, but it's not. Suppose you are walking down a road and come to a fork in the road, but the road does not split off into two roads but many different roads. Each of the many roads represents a whole new world of possibilities, but which road do we choose?

The road we choose represents the choice we make, and as we walk down that road we don't know what lies ahead; that's what Atkinson' novel is all about—the many roads that Ursula Todd took. When she dies in one life she is reborn into the same life, which brings her to the many forks in the road again, and again, and again— hence the many parallel lives of Ursula Todd. That's why Atkinson called her novel *Life after Life*.

At first glance one would think that the title refers to the life we will live on the other side of the veil of life when we die, which

Dr. Raymond Moody wrote about in his book by the same title, *Life after Life*; but that's not what Atkinson meant. She meant that one lives the same life over again lifetime after lifetime in the Nietzschean sense of the eternal recurrence of the same life, but with a twist—the twist being that we can change the course of our same life by taking a different fork in the road.

It follows that CHOICE is Atkinson's theme. She wants to see how choice affects our same life over and over again; and the somewhat nebulous conclusion that she arrives at with her highly imaginative narratives of Ursula Todd's many parallel lives is that somehow things get better with repetition. By repeating her life over and over again her heroine gets a little bit better and better at being Ursula Todd—a fascinating creative insight that I simply have to explore in today's spiritual musing…

The problem that I have with Atkinson's novel is that the serpent keeps swallowing its tail. In one of her lives, Ursula's parents take her to a psychiatrist at the age of ten, and her sessions with the doctor touch upon the subject of reincarnation. She is moody and spacey, and her doctor asks her to draw something, and she draws a serpent swallowing its tail. Her doctor explains the drawing: "Time is a construct, in reality everything flows, no past or present, only now." The serpent swallowing its tail symbolizes eternal return.

Ursula Todd keeps living the same life over again in parallel worlds, and each life has a different outcome; but to what end? Is Ursula Todd destined to keep repeating her life over and over again (albeit with different outcomes) forever in the NOW of reality. This is the central mystery of the novel (and life) that Atkinson does not resolve. The only resolution she offers is that with repetition things get better. But again, to what end?

Strangely enough, I just finished writing the story of my own parallel life. My book is called *The Summoning of Noman, The True Story of My Parallel Life;* and in my story I offer a resolution to the mystery of the eternal return.

Apparently, I had lived my life as Orest Stocco once; but because I was not happy with the outcome of my life I chose to return to my same life to live over again for the specific purpose of achieving a different outcome. I was told this by the Ascended Master St. Padre Pio during one of my spiritual healing sessions.

St. Padre Pio was channeled by a gifted psychic medium (she channeled the Ascended Master consciously, not in a trance), and he informed me that my current life is my parallel life; that's why I had to write the story of how I broke the eternal cycle of reincarnation—which was the outcome that I came to achieve this time around.

Kate Atkinson caught a glimpse of our purpose in life by indicating that with repetition things get better; but she does not tell us to what end, thereby leaving us with the dread of the eternal recurrence of life—because with each parallel life that we live we can make different choices and thereby create an endless stream of parallel lives for the parallel lives that we live—a never-ending continuum of parallel lives!

The writer Paul Twitchell said, "If you don't get it right in this life, you will just keep coming back until you do." That's what Atkinson's novel hints at with her insight that with repetition things get better; and as fascinating as the narratives of Ursula Todds parallel lives are to read, they leave one standing on the edge of a mystery that one can spend their whole life trying to resolve.

This mystery can be summed up by the question the Preacher asks in the Book of Ecclesiastes: *"what profit hath a man of all his labor which he taketh under the sun?"* It doesn't matter how many lives we live, parallel or not, we will all come to that point in our life when we ask the dreaded question: what is the purpose of life?

Kate Atkinson can't tell us. She spins a wonderful tale of parallel lives, but she can't penetrate the mystery. That's why I wrote the true story of my parallel life. So, just what is the answer to this dreaded question?

"Vanity of vanities, all is vanity," said the Preacher, indicating that unless we know the purpose of life we will be living it in vain. This is why Socrates said that the unexamined life was not worth living, and he spent his whole life trying to make sense of why we are here. So what if we come back into our same life to live over again, or if we reincarnate into a different body to live a new life; what is the purpose of our life?

As presumptuous as this may sound, I found the answer. It wasn't out there waiting to be found, though: I had to initiate myself into the mystery of life. And that's what my story *The Summoning of Noman, The True Story of My Parallel Life* is all about.

Suffice to say that the answer to the dreaded question is this: we are born for the specific purpose of expanding the consciousness of God by realizing our divine nature; and we realize our divine nature by taking evolution into our own hands to complete what Nature cannot accomplish, because Nature's purpose is to evolve soul to the point where soul must take responsibility for its own destiny; and the only way we can do that is to live the Way consciously, because the more conscious we become of the Way the more the mystery of life's purpose is revealed to us. But, as Jesus tells us, **"strait is the gate, and narrow is the way, which leadeth unto life, and few there be who find it."**

Atkinson's novel *Life after Life* is a wonderful read, but it doesn't do much to solve the mystery of life; that's a personal responsibility, because as Gurdjieff said, "There is only self-initiation into the mysteries of life." As simple as it may sound, we keep coming back until we get life right; and getting life right means not creating the kind of karma that keeps us trapped in the cycle of the eternal return. And how do we do that?

Well, that's the real mystery, isn't it?

25. The Special Message of Story

I was driving into Waverly to pick up my Saturday *Post*—I go out of my way to read Conrad Black's column every weekend, and there are only two places in this area of Georgian Bay that bring in the *National Post*, the paper that Conrad Black founded but later sold; I read his weekly column because I love how he's reclaiming his personal honor after time served in a Florida prison for being found guilty of fraud and obstruction of justice—and I was thinking of the fourth chapter of my "forgotten novel" that I had just finished editing when the idea for today's spiritual musing struck me like a bolt out of the clear blue—***the special message of story!***

Let me explain. Sometime last year I went to my basement "library" (most of my five thousand books are still packed in boxes from our move to Georgian Bay) looking for a specific book on dreams (Patricia Garflield's *Creative Dreaming*) when for some reason I was strongly nudged to go through one of my plastic storage containers of manuscripts, and to my surprise I found a novel that I had completely forgotten I had written thirteen years ago; so I brought it upstairs and set the grey binder on top of a box of papers and other binders in my writing den where it sat until I brought my new book *The Summoning of Noman* to closure, and the next morning I began reading my forgotten novel.

My novel was called "Grace," but during the editing process the story gave birth to a new title, *Tea with Grace, A Story of Synchronicity and Platonic Love,* which best captures the relationship that my narrator, a housepainter and creative writer, has with the woman whose house he was painting, an ex nun who married an ex monk; and in the fourth chapter my narrator explains why he and Grace are magnetically attracted to each other.

Grace has a story to tell. It is *her* story. And her painter Oriano also has a story to tell. It is *his* story; and both stories are so distinctive that they become fascinated by each other's story and cannot seem to get enough of each other as they disclose bits and pieces of their life story while he's painting her house and over morning and afternoon tea.

That's what I was thinking about on my drive to Waverly; but my writer's mind being what it is, I naturally associated Grace and Oriano's compulsion to tell their story to the creative writer's compulsion to write stories, and I exclaimed to myself—*"That's why writers **have** to write; they're compelled by the power of story to write!"*

It's always been a mystery why writers have to write; but for some reason known only to the creative unconscious, when all the relevant aspects of an idea come together in the unconscious and coalesce into a seed idea that has to take root in the conscious mind of the writer, it will break through and **compel** the writer to give it life in a story—just as grass is compelled to break through asphalt to take in the light of the sun.

That's what happened on my drive to Waverly Saturday morning; all the relevant factors came together to coalesce into the seed idea for today's spiritual musing. But this is such an elusive idea that I will need all the help I can get to bring it to light; and so I call upon my Muse to explain *the special message of story*.

As always, whenever I write a spiritual musing I have to have an entry point; so I sat back and let my mind wander until it occurred to me why Grace and Oriano felt compelled to tell their story, and I went to chapter four of my forgotten novel to locate the passage that I *knew* would be a perfect point of entry into *the special message of story*:

"Not everyone has this compulsive need to tell their story, only certain people; and Grace was one. Whatever it was that made her what she was, she had to share it with someone because deep in her soul she knew that it was worth sharing. But it wasn't simply a matter of wanting to share one's story because it was worth sharing; there was something about their life that compelled them to share it, as though one had a *special message* that the world had to hear; and Grace and I had a *special message* to share."

The key phrase is *special message*. My Muse highlighted this phrase because it goes to the heart of the mystery of story; but to articulate what I mean by *special message* I have to go way out there and circle my way back; but where to start?

STUPIDITY IS NOT A GIFT OF GOD

One of the factors that came together to coalesce into the seed of my musing idea today was the revelation that Doctor Jung had while working in the Burgholzli Psychiatric Hospital in Zurich. It came to him while listening to his patients that despite what sounded like incoherent nonsense, his patients all had a story to tell; and because their story got interrupted they lost their way and ended up in the mental hospital. Jung saw that if he could get his patients to reconnect with their life story they could be healed.

This was the "key" to the mystery of mental illness that Jung was looking for, because he realized that reconnecting his patients with their life story would reconnect them with their life purpose; which led to his famous word association test and birth of analytical psychology. Jung later discovered with his own soul-searching experience, which he recorded in his private journals that were to become his legendary *Red Book,* that **"life is the way, the long sought-after way to the unfathomable, which we call divine,"** and only by living one's life's story could one fulfill their life purpose.

But why? What is it about living one's own life that connects one with the meaning and purpose of their life? This is the mystery of story, because **one's life is the way to the unfathomable, to the divine**; which is what motivated Jung to create a psychology of individuation to help his patients reconnect with their life story. But because everyone's life is unique to him or her, their story would be different; hence, their *special message* and why the Sufis say that there are as many paths to God as there are souls of man.

When Jesus was asked by the Pharisees when the kingdom of God would come, he replied: *"The kingdom of God does not come with outward signs to be observed. Nor will they say, 'Look here!' or 'Look over there!' For behold, the kingdom of God is within you and around you"* (Luke 17: 20-21). "Kingdom of God" was Christ's metaphor for the Way, which is everywhere to be found because the Way is Divine Spirit, the life force and omniscient guiding force of life; and when we bring our karmic destiny into alignment with our spiritual destiny we connect with the Way, the path to our true self.

Which means that the more true we are to ourselves, the more we live the Way. This is what Jung realized, because in his own "confrontation with the unconscious" he reclaimed his lost soul by bringing his outer life back into alignment with his spiritual destiny;

and the psychology that he forged out of his "confrontation with the unconscious" became *the special message* of his life story and invaluable legacy to the world.

    When I got home Saturday morning I spent the next three hours on the front deck reading the *National Post*, starting with Conrad Black's column, because I *knew* that there was a ***special message*** in his distinct life story (newspaper baron, historian, and biographer), whatever topic his columns were about (I especially love them when he's in an iconoclastic frame of mind because it unleashes his lethal vocabulary); a message that spoke to what Dr. Maurice Nicoll, who studied under Doctor Jung in Zurich before taking up G. I. Gurdjieff's special teaching of self-transformation in Fontainebleau, France, referred to as *"metanoia"* in his posthumous book *The Mark* (followed by *The New Man* which decodes Christ's secret teaching of self-transformation and spiritual rebirth).

    Metanoia is a Greek word, which means "change of mind" but which Dr. Nicoll in his studies of the Bible, with special attention to the New Testament, decoded to mean a transformation of self. He quotes the Bible: "…Except ye repent, ye shall all likewise perish." And he goes on to say, "The word translated throughout the New Testament as repentance is in the Greek *meta-noia,* which means change of mind," and I can't help but feel that the disgraced newspaper baron Lord Conrad Moffat Black of Crossharbour, whose Ozymandian ego was so gigantic that it took the excruciating experience of his humiliating lengthy court trial and 42 month prison sentence to level off, is undergoing a *metanoic* change of life now, which is why I love reading his weekly column—because I can *see* the repentance of his *metanoic* transformation in the private soul of his public words, and I admire and respect him for it because I believe that this is the ***special message*** of his life story and lasting legacy to the world, despite all of his other remarkable accomplishments; proving yet again that life is nothing if not a journey through vanity to humility.

26. A Bee in My Window

Synchronicity is the term created by C. G. Jung to describe the universal principle behind what he called "meaningful coincidences," which point to a higher intelligence; or what I call the omniscient guiding force of life. Synchronicity describes events that are not related in terms of cause and effect but which have meaningful psychological significance, like the experience I had when a bee flew in my partially opened window.

There's something magical about meaningful coincidences that give one a feeling of goodness, rightness, and holiness even; and every time we are blessed with such an experience we cannot help but feel that we are on the right course, like we are in sync with life. This is how Phil Cousineau describes synchronicities in his book *Soul Moments*. They are electrifying, "a visitation by a god; a palpable inrush of grace, power, and meaning; an inexplicable conviction that one is moving beyond fate and into destiny." And this is what I would like to explore in today's spiritual musing…

Although the experience I had with the bee in my window while I was typing the manuscript of my "forgotten novel" into my word processor could pass for just another experience of a bee flying into the crack between my partially opened window and screen, which happens at least two or three times every summer, this time it was different because of what I was typing; this is what made it a meaningful coincidence.

To appreciate the full flavor of this magical moment that Phil Cousineau calls a visitation by a god, let me provide the context that gave birth to the synchronistic experience of a bee flying in my window and the passage that I was typing.

The novel that I was typing into my word processor was called "Grace," but while editing and crafting it I was inspired to change the title to *Tea with Grace, A Story of Synchronicity and Platonic Love*. This title was more reflective of the relationship that my narrator Oriano Fellicci had with Grace Kendal, the married former nun who hired him to paint her house; and my new title also alluded to the popular book *Tuesdays with Morrie* by Mitch Albom that was made into a movie that both Grace and Oriano had seen.

Although *Tea with Grace* was fiction and *Tuesdays with Morrie* was the real life account of Mitch Albom's relationship with his old college professor who was dying of ALS (Lou Gehrig's disease), my novel was a fictional account of an experience I had while painting a woman's house many years ago; and the dramatic tension of my story lay in the platonic relationship that my narrator and the woman had while he worked at her house and over tea during his morning and afternoon breaks.

Grace Kendal was a nun for twenty years, and although she left her Order she had not lost her faith; and she devoted her life to serving God in the secular world. She married an ex monk and they adopted two children; and when she met Oriano she made it her mission to save his soul and bring him back to the Church.

Oriano was a Roman Catholic who left the Church in his late teens because he could not be contained by his Christian faith. He became a seeker, and by the time he met Grace Kendal he had found all the answers that he was looking for; so he was a spiritually resolved individual who could not possibly return to the teachings of the Church.

Grace however did not give up on Oriano. Ironically, the more they talked the more Grace's faith was brought into question, which creates the dramatic tension of the story; and as I was typing Chapter 8 ("A Soul Moment") a bee flew in the crack of my partially opened window and buzzed around just as I was typing in the passage where Oriano explains to Grace that she has to expand her Christian paradigm if she wanted to experience more spiritual freedom that her rigid Roman Catholic faith denied her.

The timing of the bee buzzing in my window trying to find a way out and me typing in the passage where Oriano explains to Grace that she has to expand her faith was so perfectly aligned that I experienced that magical moment called synchronicity; but to give my experience the full flavor of its synchronistic meaning I have to reference a remarkably similar coincidence that Doctor Jung experienced with one of his patients.

STUPIDITY IS NOT A GIFT OF GOD

Before I relate Jung's experience however, let me say that I felt sorry for the bee; so I cranked my window wide open so that as it flitted about the window pane looking for a way out it would hopefully fly out the much larger crack between the pane and screen that I had provided, and within a few minutes it finally found freedom. And this experience instantly brought to mind Jung's remarkable coincidence with his patient.

Jung's patient had already been to two other doctors, but they had no success with the young woman who was steeped into a Cartesian view of the world; and Jung knew that the only way he could help her to connect with her inner self so she could grow into the person she was meant to be was to break through the hard shell of her Cartesian mindset, but he had no idea how to do this. That's when the miracle of synchronicity happened.

I should mention that I've come to realize that synchronicities don't just happen out of the clear blue, as many people believe; they are manifested by the omniscient guiding force of life to assist us in our individuation process whenever we get stuck on our journey to wholeness, like Jung's patient and the former nun in my novel *Tea with Grace*.

Jung's patient could not become the woman she was born to be because her Cartesian mindset inhibited her individuation process, and the only way Jung could make any progress with her was to expand her belief system; which is what Oriano was trying to do with Grace Kendal. But both Jung and Oriano could not make any progress; and so the merciful omniscient guiding force of life intervened with a synchronistic experience to clear the way for them.

In Jung's experience, his patient related a curious dream that she had of a golden scarab. "While she was telling me this dream," Jung writes in his essay on synchronicity, "I sat with my back to the closed window. Suddenly I heard a noise behind me, like a gentle tapping. I turned round and saw a flying insect knocking against the window-pane from outside. I opened the window and caught the creature in the air as it flew in. It was the nearest analogy to a golden scarab that one finds in our latitudes, a scarabaeid beetle, the common rose-chafer (*Cetonia aurata*), which contrary to its usual habits had evidently felt an urge to get into a dark room in this particular moment."

Jung goes on to say that this was an extraordinarily difficult case to treat, and up to the time of this dream little or no progress had been made because his patient's "animus, which was steeped in Cartesian philosophy and clung so rigidly to its own idea of reality the efforts of three doctors—and I was the third—had not been able to weaken it....evidently something quite irrational was needed which was beyond my powers to produce," wrote Jung. "The dream alone was enough to disturb ever so slightly the rationalistic attitude of my patient. But when the 'scarab' came flying through the window in actual fact, her natural being could burst through the armour of her animus possession and the process of transformation could at last begin to move" (S*ynchronicity, An Acausal Connecting Principle*, by C.G. Jung, Bollingen Series XX, pp. 22-23).

In the chapter that I was typing when the bee flew in the crack of my window and couldn't get out, Oriano revealed to Grace the remarkable coincidence that he experienced in Chapters book store over the weekend when the book *Soul Moments* fell off the shelf to the floor in front of his feet which he picked up and learned that Phil Cousineau called synchronicities "Soul moments," and Oriano explained to Grace that he believed they had been brought together by the "gods of synchronicity" so he could break down her rigid faith which denied her the spiritual freedom that her anguished soul longed for.

Just as Jung's remarkable coincidence of his patient's dream of the golden scarab and the beetle that flew into the room broke down his patients Cartesian mindset to help set her free, so did Oriano break down Grace's rigid faith with every discourse they had so she could be set free of the hold that her Roman Catholic faith had upon her. This is why I saw the bee that flew in my window at precisely the time that I was typing in the passage where Oriano is trying to expand Grace's faith as a remarkable coincidence similar to Jung's experience with his patient. Jung's coincidence freed up his patient so the transformation process could begin to work in her life, and Oriano opened up the window of Grace's soul so the transformation process could begin to work in her life. As I opened my window wider so the trapped bee could escape and fly to freedom, so did Oriano expand Grace's faith with every discourse they had while he painted her house. Oriano opened the window of Grace's soul, as it were; but would she fly to freedom as the bee in my window?

To find out one will have to read the novel…

27. The Conversion Experience

This is a spiritual musing that I wanted to write twenty years ago, long before I came up with the idea of writing spiritual musings; it was my insight into the experience that people have of going from one extreme to the other—from non-belief to belief. But then I read Dr. Eben Alexander's book *Proof of Heaven,* and I felt compelled to write a spiritual musing on the conversion experience…

I came upon Dr. Alexander's miraculous NDE (near-death experience) on You Tube several months before I purchased his book *Proof of Heaven.* I was impressed by his story because it was the best example of an NDE that I had ever seen, and I went on Amazon to check out his book; but I didn't order it right away.

I had many other books to read for the book that I was writing (*The Summoning of Noman*), so I waited; and then one day last week I just "happened" to spot *Proof of Heaven* on the discount table in Wal-Mart and I felt compelled to buy it; and after I finished reading *The Uncertain Art, Thoughts on a Life in Medicine,* by Dr. Sherwin B. Nuland (which I loved for his wisdom and compassion) I read Dr. Alexander's book in two sittings.

Proof of Heaven is a fascinating conversion experience story, but it was not the first that I had come across. I had heard and read of many conversion stories, my favorite being Dr. Brian L. Weiss's experience which he recounts in his book *Many Lives, Many Masters.* This is the story of his conversion from a non-believer in past lives to a believer in past lives; and today he is one of the world's foremost practitioners of past-life regression therapy, holding workshops that attract hundreds of people. But as compelling as Dr. Weiss's conversion experience was, it cannot compare to Dr. Alexander's.

Dr. Eben Alexander was a scientist first and foremost, believing that biology was the creator of consciousness (meaning, the brain creates consciousness); but after he was struck by bacterial meningitis and went into a coma for seven days and had his near-death experience he converted from a non-believer into a believer, and today he's on a mission to prove to the world that our consciousness exists apart from our brain and that Heaven is real—and by Heaven Dr. Alexander means higher states of consciousness.

Proof of Heaven is categorical proof of Gurdjieff's comment that **there is only self-initiation into the mysteries of life**; because had Dr. Alexander not had his NDE he would have continued his life believing that our brain creates the matrix of consciousness that we call the self—that mysterious individuated state of consciousness we call "I" which continues to exist after our body dies.

What makes Dr. Alexander's NDE stand out from all other near-death experiences are two things: 1. the fact that he is a scientist; a neurosurgeon, to be exact; and 2. the very nature of his NDE, which is so well-defined that it offers the most conclusive proof to date that consciousness exists apart from the brain.

Before his conversion NDE, Dr. Alexander believed that "the brain is the machine that produces consciousness (and) when the machine breaks down consciousness stops." But then he contracted the mysterious virus that sent him into a seven day coma that was responsible for his OBE (out-of-body experience) that made a believer out of him.

"During my coma my brain wasn't working improperly—it wasn't working *at all*," he writes in *Proof of Heaven*. "…the neocortex (the outer surface of the brain, the part that makes us human) was out of the picture. I was encountering the reality of a world of consciousness that existed *completely free of the limitations of my physical brain.* Mine was in some ways a perfect storm of near-death experiences. As a practicing neurosurgeon with decades of research and hands-on work in the operating room behind me, I was in a better-than-average person to judge not only the reality but also the implications of what happened to me...My experience showed me that the death of the body and the brain are not the end of consciousness, that human experience continues beyond the grave" (p. 9).

His NDE was so dramatic that Dr. Alexander did a complete about-face and reversed his position from believing that without the brain consciousness does not exist to the belief that consciousness exists apart from the brain—a position that is argued with scientific conviction by quantum physicist Amit Goswamin in his book *The*

Self-Aware Universe, How Consciousness Creates the Material World.

Dr. Eben Alexander is not just anybody, then; he is a reputable neurosurgeon whose credibility cannot be dismissed. That's what makes his NDE so convincing and why he is doing the talk show circuit and his book *Proof of Heaven* is taken so seriously.

I certainly don't have the academic credentials to bolster my credibility like Dr. Alexander, but his NDE leads me to introduce my own out-of-body experience in which I experienced the deepest part of Heaven where all souls are created before they are sent by God into the material worlds to begin their journey through life for the specific purpose of realizing their own individual identity—that matrix of consciousness we call "I".

Whether one believes my OBE or not is immaterial to me, because like Gurdjieff (and Dr. Eben Alexander) I know from personal experience that there is only self-initiation into the mysteries of life; but my OBE sheds light upon the impenetrable mystery of consciousness and the self that I would also like to share with the world…

Shortly after Penny and I moved to Georgian Bay eight years ago I had seven past-life regressions, and in my fourth regression I was brought back to the Body of God where all souls come from; and in this regression I experienced myself as an atom of God with Soul consciousness but no self-consciousness. I was a soul without identity.

In this same regression I was sent from the Body of God down into the lower worlds of consciousness; specifically, this Earth world. And I was sent here with the *a priori* purpose of acquiring my own identity through the natural process of evolution.

So there I was, an atom of God (an un-self-realized soul seed) evolving up the ladder of natural evolution collecting and constellating the life-force (the consciousness of life) through countless lower life-form incarnations of plants and animals until my incarnation as a higher primate which constelled enough life-consciousness to reach critical mass and become aware of itself for the very first time, and in my regression I actually *experienced* the dawning of my own reflective self-consciousness.

As impossible as it may be to believe, I experienced the birth of my own "I"—my individual identity; and with each new incarnation I grew in self-realization consciousness until in my current lifetime I was evolved enough to take the natural process of unconscious evolution through karma and reincarnation into my own hands with Gurfjieff's teaching of "work on oneself" and the sayings of Jesus and I gave birth to my spiritual self.

This was my self-initiation experience into the deepest mystery of life—the very purpose of our existence, which is to give birth to a new "I" of God.

This is not to say that I or any other self is God; we are and we aren't. We are all made of the same divine stuff, which is the consciousness of life. When Moses asked God on Mount Sinai to define himself, God replied "I Am that I Am. And whenever an atom of God gives birth to its own identity, as I experienced in my regression, it gives birth to a new "I" of God—hence, we are all God insomuch that we are made of the same divine stuff.

This led me to the realization that God created life so God could grow in the consciousness of God through natural evolution, and that man is central to expanding the consciousness of God—hence, "I Am *that* I Am."

Dr. Eben Alexander was unexpectedly initiated into the mystery that consciousness exists apart from the brain when he was infected with bacterial meningitis and had an NDE that proves conclusively that we are more than our body, but the journey of self-realization consciousness does not stop there; the next stage is ***conscious evolution,*** and this can only happen when one steps up to the plate and takes karmic responsibility for his own life.

Nature can only evolve us so far through the unconscious process of natural evolution (karma and reincarnation), and to realize our *a priori* purpose as spiritual beings we have to take evolution into our own hands. This is what Dr. Alexander's conversion experience awakens us to; and I for one am delighted that he wrote *Proof of Heaven.*

I still marvel however at how the gods of synchronicity brought me to the book bargain bin at Wal-Mart last week when I had no intention of going there; but that's material for another musing on the omniscient guiding force of life…

28. A Cheap Shot at Shirley MacLaine

A couple of weeks ago I was browsing through my books in one of the bookcases in our sun room just off the kitchen, where I do most of my reading in the winter because I can put on a nice fire in our Pacific wood stove and enjoy the cozy heat and dancing flames, when Ken Wilber's book grabbed my attention; and I *knew* that I had to read it.

I do this every so often, about once a month; I browse through my bookcases to see which book jumps out at me. This is one way that I open myself up to the omniscient guiding force of life, because the books that I am nudged to read will tell me if I'm still in sync with my destined purpose in life, or if I should be going in another direction.

The books that I am nudged to read never take me in a dramatic new direction, because I have found my path in life, which is the Way; but being an individual path, the Way demands that we explore little side roads every so often to satisfy our spiritual needs, answer some of our unanswered questions, and add to our understanding of life. That's what Ken Wilber's book *Eye to Eye, The Quest for the New Paradigm* did for me.

I wasn't nudged to read Wilber's book to answer any unanswered questions (I don't have any at the moment, believe it or not), but to add to my understanding of life and satisfy my need to know; and I needed to know where Ken Wilber stood in his journey through life, because he is unquestionably one of the most brilliant writers on the perennial philosophy of life—or, if you will, the inherent wisdom of the spiritual traditions both east and west; and *Eye to Eye* was a good place to start, because in this book Wilber sought to bring all paths into one paradigm that embraced all known traditions of the Way.

Of course, I had no idea why I was nudged to read Wilber's book after all this time (it had been quietly sitting on my shelf ever since we moved to Georgian Bay nine years ago); but I soon realized that I had been nudged to bring resolution to my understanding of reincarnation and the Buddhist perspective on reincarnation; and because Ken Wilbur embraced the Buddhist perspective it was time to satisfy my need to know exactly where I stood with respect to Buddhism, because if anyone could give a clear explanation of where Buddhism stood on reincarnation, Ken Wilber would be the man—aside from the Dalai Lama, whose book I had just finished reading (*The Art of Happiness*, *A Handbook for Living*, by the Dalai Lama and Howard C. Cutler, M.D.).

But *Eye to Eye* was not an easy book to read. In fact, truth be told, I could not read the whole book. I read the *Forward* by Frances Vaughan, *Preface to the Third Edition, Revised,* by the author Ken Wilber, the first chapter "Eye to Eye," skim read through all the other chapters, and then read the last chapter "The Ultimate State of Consciousness" and the *Epilogue*. But it was the last chapter that brought the book home for me, because it summed up where Wilber stood in his understanding of the Way. To quote his summation:

"Throughout this volume we have pointed out that the Absolute is both the highest state of being and the ground of all being; it is both the goal of evolution and the ground of evolution; the highest stage of development and the reality or suchness of all stages of development; the highest of all conditions and the Condition of all conditions; the highest rung on the ladder *and* the wood out of which the entire ladder is made. Anything less than that *paradox* generates either pantheistic reductionism, on the one hand, or wild and radical transcendentalism, on the other" (*Eye to Eye*, p. 266).

As elaborately expressed as it is, this resonated with me; and if I were to reduce all of this into one sentence it would be this: the Way just IS!

Ken Wilber knows this, but he has a need to give his understanding of the Way the most comprehensive intellectual expression possible. Nonetheless this did not satisfy my need to know where Buddhism stood on reincarnation; so I went on You Tube and listened to Wilber's talk on the Buddhist perspective on reincarnation. His talk is titled "Conscious Reincarnation," and as I listened I heard what I needed to satisfy my need to know exactly why my understanding of reincarnation differed from the Buddhist perspective; but because of the cheap shot that Wilber gave to Shirley

MacLaine I felt compelled to write this musing, because Shirley MacLaine and I share the same belief in reincarnation.

This, then, is today's spiritual musing—the radical distinction between the Buddhist perspective on reincarnation, and mine and Shirley MacLaine's...

Let me start by mentioning Wilber's cheap shot at Shirley MacLaine, which was said in jest but nonetheless a cheap shot that poked fun at her belief in reincarnation.

Ken Wilber is asked a question by a female member of the audience about conscious reincarnation, and he replies: "Reincarnation is a very, very, very difficult topic…The Dalai Lama says he can't remember his past lives; Shirley MacLaine can (laughter from Wilber and the audience). So already we've got a little bit of a problem, if you know what I mean."

Why would Wilber laugh at the fact that Shirley MacLaine says she can remember her past lives and the Dalai Lama can't (which I doubt, by the way; I suspect he has just spun memories of his past lives to fit into his Buddhist paradigm), if not to measure Shirley MacLaine's belief system with the Dalai Lama's, leaving the audience to draw the subjective conclusion that the Dalai Lama is more credible than Shirley MacLaine? But is the Dalai Lama more credible? That's the question I want to explore in today's musing.

It is very easy to be intimidated by a person's stature—be it the spiritual stature of His Holiness the Dalai Lama, the daunting intellectual stature of a writer like Ken Wilber, or the imposing stature of a great novelist, poet, artist, actor, musician, scientist, or political reformer like Nelson Mandela; but I dropped out of university in my third year of philosophy studies because I came to the disconcerting realization that the only truth I could really depend upon in the end was the truth of my own experiences, and with Gurdjieff's teaching of self-transformation under my arm I left university and went out into the world to initiate myself into the mysteries of life through my daily interactions with life.

Without realizing it, I chose to live what can simply be called "the gnostic way of life," which is the natural path of experience; and the more I experienced life within the paradigm of Gurdjieff's teaching of "work on oneself," the more I initiated myself into the mysteries of life until I awakened to the Way (the inherently self-transcending power of Holy Spirit that flows through life), which I began to live consciously. And when I was ready for the answer to the perennial question of life *(who am I?)* I had seven past-life regressions that initiated me into the divine mystery of soul's primary purpose in life, which automatically set me apart from the Buddhist perspective on reincarnation.

The best explanation of the Buddhist perspective on reincarnation that I have ever come across comes from the book *The Monk and the Philosopher*, by Jean-Francois Revel and his son Matthiew Ricard. Although Ken Wilber reflects this perspective in his talk, I want to quote what the Tibetan monk Matthiew Ricard has to say about reincarnation:

"First of all, it's important to understand that what's called reincarnation in Buddhism has nothing to do with the transmigration of some 'entity' or other. It's not a process of metempsychosis because there is no 'soul'. As long as one thinks in terms of entities rather than function and continuity, it's impossible to understand the Buddhist concept of rebirth. As it's said, 'There is no thread passing through the beads of the necklace of rebirths.' Over successive rebirths, what is maintained is not the identity of a 'person', but the conditioning of a stream of consciousness."

Matthiew Ricard's explanation of reincarnation puzzles his journalist/philosopher father Jean-Francois Revel, who responds, "A series of reincarnations without any definite entity that reincarnates? More and more mysterious."

To help his father understand, Matthiew offers an analogy to explain the Buddhist perspective on reincarnation: "It could be likened to a river without a boat descending along its course, or to a lamp that lights a second lamp, which in turn lights a third lamp, and so on; the flame at the end of the process is neither the same flame as at the outset, nor a completely different one" (*The Monk and the Philosopher*, pp. 30-31).

Ken Wilber simplifies this by saying that there is only one self called *I Am*, and what reincarnates is this *I Am*; so the concept of an individual self that reincarnates from one life to the next is illusory, and Matthiew Ricard enforces this view: "Buddhism accepts that there is a continuum of consciousness, but denies any existence of a solid, permanent, and autonomous self anywhere in that continuum. ***The essence of Buddhist practice is therefore to get rid of that illusion of self which so falsifies our view of the world***" (p. 35, bold italics mine).

"That illusion of self" is the reason for Ken Wilber's cheap shot at Shirley MacLaine, because what he's really saying is that she's fooling herself to believe that she is an individual autonomous self that reincarnates from one life to the next; but what if I were to say that I have proof that Shirley MacLaine's perspective is valid? What if I were to say that I have experienced the birth of my own individual self, and that I have experienced the growth of my individual self from one life to the next? Would this not draw a clear distinction between the Buddhist perspective and Shirley MacLaine's and mine? Which is not to say that the Buddhist perspective is invalid; it only says that Buddhism only offers one half of the story on reincarnation. So, if I may, let me offer the other half...

I had seven past-life regressions eight years ago because I wanted to prove for myself that my current life was influenced by my past lives. My inspiration for having my regressions came from the author Jess Stern (*Edgar Cayce: the Sleeping Prophet*) whose fascinating book on the historical novelist's past lives excited my curiosity about my own past lives (*The Search for the Soul: Psychic Lives of Taylor Caldwell*); but I got more than what I had bargained for with my regressions. Not only did I get the proof that I was looking for, because I was brought back to my past lives that had the most influence upon my current life; I also got proof of the existence of the individual Soul self!

In my fourth regression I was brought back to the Body of God, or what in one ancient spiritual tradition is poetically referred to as the Ocean of Love and Mercy; and I experienced myself as an atom in the Body of God, very much like a single drop of water in the ocean. But the strange thing about my experience was that I did not have self-consciousness. I had Soul consciousness, but no self-consciousness; and the only reason I know this is because I was my evolved self experiencing myself in the Body of God where I had come from before I was sent out into the lower worlds to grow and evolve and create my own individual self-consciousness. And in the same regression I experienced myself in the world evolving up the evolutionary ladder of life from the lowest life form all the way up to my lifetime as a higher primate (I was the alpha male of a group of ten or twelve members) where I experienced the dawning of my self-consciousness!

I actually experienced the birth of my own reflective self-consciousness; and I continued to evolve in my individual self-consciousness from lifetime to lifetime until I took evolution into my own hands in my current life by living the Way consciously with Gurdjieff's teaching and the sayings of Jesus, and one day I gave birth to my spiritual self in my mother's kitchen while she was kneading dough on the kitchen table. Quietly, unexpectedly I experienced the birth of my spiritual self and I *knew* that I was Soul!

But I need not go into detail in this musing because I've already done this in my novel *Cathedral of My Past Lives.* Suffice to say that my past-life regressions validate both perspectives on reincarnation; or, if you will, the Buddhist *I Am* perspective and the individual Soul self perspective, which are both expressed in the *I Am that I Am* first-cause principle, thereby completing the story on the divine mystery of reincarnation.

So the Buddhist perspective is valid, because the universal self of God (the "I" of God) evolves through life and reincarnates from one life form to the next until it inhabits a life form that will be evolved enough to become aware of itself in the birth of a new "I" of God, as I experienced in my regression; and the birth of my reflective self validates the individual Soul self perspective on reincarnation, as Shirley MacLaine and I believe—hence, *I Am* THAT *I Am*. This is why after I gave birth to my spiritual self I wrote in my journal, **"I am what I am not, and I am not what I am; I am both, but neither: I am Soul,"** and why Paul Twitchell, the modern day founder of the ancient spiritual teachings of The Way of the Eternal, wrote that God needs man as much as man needs God.

There is much more to this story, of course; but I will leave that for my essay at the end of my book—"A Personal Essay on the Evolutionary Impulse to Individuate: A Response to the Spiritual Path of Evolutionary Enlightenment."

29. An Exercise in Active Imagination

Today's spiritual musing was born of an exercise in "active imagination," a creative technique that I engage in every so often to play out an idea that craves to be expressed, very much like writing a scene in a novel and giving my characters all the creative freedom they need to be who they are; and the idea that I wanted to play out was the claim made by a New Age spiritual path (the Way of the Eternal) that it is "the most direct path to God."

"That's one perspective," I said, to the short Bette Midler look-alike who made this claim in my imaginary scenario. "It's valid for you, because that's what you choose to believe; but as Neale Donald Walsh said in *Home with God*, his last public conversation with God, 'No path back Home is better than any other.' I know you don't claim this path to be better, only the most direct; but all souls exist in the eternal NOW and are thereby equidistant from God. Given this perspective, no path to God is more direct than any other path; they are all the same distance, if you follow the logic. As God tells Neale, 'Your perspective is your perception.' And by this he meant that what you believe creates your reality. So in the end it all boils down to this: what path is best for me?"

"How would one know that?" a serious-looking lady in her mid fifties asked. She had come to our monthly spiritual function at the public library of my mind to find out what this "most direct path to God" was all about. A seeker for the last ten years of her life (which began with the accidental drowning of her daughter in the family swimming pool), she never found a path that "spoke" to her, and she was testing the waters one more time. I saw the longing in her eyes, and I felt the anguish of her soul.

"That all depends," I said, and no sooner did I say this and I felt the strongest urge to let Soul speak—which was the whole purpose of my active imagination exercise, to connect with my higher Self; so I abandoned to my creative unconscious and let Soul say what it had to say to resolve the perplexing issue of finding one's right spiritual path.

"Depends on what?" she asked.

"On how honest you are with yourself," I replied.

"What does that mean?" she asked, with a puzzled look.

"How much do you trust your own intuition?" I answered, and instantly I felt grabbed by the creative impulse of my imagination and I knew that I was in for an exciting new spiritual insight—which was the whole point of my exercise, and the reason why I've come to believe that the creative act of the imagination is the most natural and satisfying path to what Carl Jung's dream teacher called "wholeness and singleness of self."

The lady stared at me, too puzzled to be offended by the implication of my comment that she was not honest enough with herself to find the right path. "I don't see the connection," she said. "Are you saying—*what are you saying, exactly?*"

I smiled at her confusion. "In my book *What Would I Say Today If I Were To Die Tomorrow?* I wrote, **'Self-deception is our greatest threat to personal growth, happiness, and wholeness.'** Please don't take this personally, but our capacity for intuitive insight is directly related to how much we trust ourselves. The less we trust ourselves, the more confused we're going to be. You asked me how one would know if a spiritual path is right for them, like this spiritual path that you came here today to explore; is the Way of the Eternal right for you or not? Can you tell?"

"Are you asking me?"

"Yes."

"I'm not sure. I haven't made up my mind yet."

"And how would you make up your mind? I presume this isn't the first spiritual teaching that you've looked into?"

"No. I've looked into many teachings."

"And you haven't found a path you like yet?"

"Not yet."

"So you're still looking; why?"

"None of the paths that I looked into spoke to me."

"And by that I take it to mean that you didn't hear what you needed to hear to satisfy the longing you have in your soul?"

STUPIDITY IS NOT A GIFT OF GOD

"That's a good way of putting it. No, I didn't hear what I needed to hear."

"Obviously, it's a question of resonance. Does a path resonate with you or not? This speaks to the Sufi saying that there are as many paths to God as there are souls of man. This means that every soul is its own path home to God, but a person has to connect with their inner self to find their path; and that's what the quest for spiritual paths is all about—finding out which path will help you connect with your inner self."

"That's what I'd like to know," said the lady, with a glimmer of hope in her eyes.

"Have you checked out Carolyn Myss's work?" I asked.

"I've come across her books, but I haven't read her yet. Why?"

"I'd suggest you start with her book *Sacred Contracts*. It spells out how you can become conscious of your individual purpose in life—or sacred contract, as she calls it; because that's what you're looking for. You want to know what your purpose is; right?"

"Yes, I think so. That's why I'm here. If I may ask you, what path are you on?"

"I embrace all teachings, but this path is my anchor teaching."

"Can you explain that for me, please?" the lady asked, her eyes imploring me.

I smiled at her need to know, and being true to my calling I to decided to bare myself to her. "To use your metaphor, this path speaks to me the loudest," I replied; "but that doesn't mean that other paths don't speak to me. Every path speaks the Way; but as Jesus would say, do you have eyes to see? Most people don't, because they're not ready for the Way. That's why Jesus also said, '**Many are called but few are chosen.**' Gurdjieff said that Nature will only evolve us so far, and then we have to take evolution into our own hands; which implies that if we're not evolved enough to take evolution into our own hands we will not hear the Way when it speaks to us, regardless which path we look into. And as silly as this may sound, we only hear the Way when we hear it; which is why some people will tell you that they just happened to come upon their path by pure chance. They didn't know it, but they were ready for the

Way; and the divine law of synchronicity arranged for them to find their path. That's what happened to me. Not once, but several times."

"I don't understand," said the lady, now more confused than ever.

I tried to explain the mystery of the natural process of individuation: "It all depends upon the individual, but a person can outgrow their path. I found Gurdjieff's teaching while studying philosophy at university; but after living his teaching for a number of years I outgrew it, so the divine law of synchronicity once again arranged for me to find the path best suited to my new state of consciousness. And thirty years later, here I am. That's how life works; when the student is ready, the teacher appears…"

I ended my active imagination exercise and went out to get my weekend papers—the *National Post* and *Globe and Mail*; but on my drive into Midland I reflected on my imaginary scenario, and it all seemed to boil down to a question of self-honesty.

"If we're not honest with ourselves, how can we connect with our inner self?" I reflected; and no sooner did I ask the question and the archetypal lady seeker popped back into the public library of my mind where we were having our imaginary talk—

"What does that have to do with finding a spiritual path that speaks to me?" she asked, responding to my spontaneous reflection. "I don't see the connection."

I paused to let my mind go blank, and then I let Soul speak: "It has everything to do with it, because if we're not honest with ourselves we can't hear the little voice within. How many times have we been nudged to do something only to regret that we didn't pay attention to our silent little voice? And when we did pay attention, weren't we thankful for paying attention because it proved to be the right thing to do? That little voice within is our higher Self speaking to us, but we can't hear it if we aren't honest with ourselves."

I could feel the lady's unease. "I'm honest with myself," she responded, rather nervously. "If I wasn't, I probably would have fallen for any number of teachings."

"Perhaps," I replied, now in full command of my scenario. "Skepticism can work against you as much as it can work for you. Self-honesty demands a certain responsibility that we may not want to assume, and rather than take on the responsibility demanded of us when we listen to our little voice we may justify ourselves to avoid the responsibility. For example, I was introduced to a spiritual path that proved to be the right path for me, but the only reason I looked into this path was because I had the wisdom to override my ego and listen to my inner voice. Let me explain. I thought that the woman who introduced me to the Way of the Eternal was a genuine flake, so how could I take what she had to say seriously? But I put my ego aside and looked into this path because I was nudged to do so, and wouldn't you know it—*it was exactly the right path for me!* In a word, my little voice insisted that I look into this path, but my ego didn't want me to because it judged this lady to be too idiosyncratic to be taken seriously; and thankfully I listened to my little voice."

This gave my imaginary lady seeker something to think about; but that was only my scenario, conjured up in the womb of my active imagination—*and how real could that be?* That's when synchronicity kicked in to validate my new creative insight…

I picked up my papers at the Super Store in Midland, plus a few groceries, and came home. Penny and I had lunch, and then she continued with her housework and I sat on the front deck to "work" my papers, as Penny likes to say because I spend hours reading my weekend papers to stay abreast of the unfolding consciousness of our times—true to the imperative that I got from Jesus in Glenda Green's book *Love without End, Jesus Speaks:* **"Simply follow life and the living. Do not follow the dead and dying. By this I mean do not adapt to ways of life, structures, ideas, concepts, or businesses which are becoming ineffective and obsolete. Look for new alignments, opportunities, and understandings which refresh your life. The whole universe is built around a priority for life and the living,"** and I always got fresh ideas and new insights from my weekend papers.

After I finished reading Conrad Black's column in the *National Post* (Saturday, July 20, 2013), which I always go to first because I love to see how he is transforming his life and reclaiming his good name, I perused the paper and came upon an article by Guest Columnist Susan Schwartz titled "Stop Pretending to like asparagus," and there it was—*synchronistic confirmation for my creative insight!*

Susan Schwartz used her dislike of asparagus as her entry point into the cognitive dissonance brought about by lack of self-honesty. "So what else have I lied to myself about?" she asks herself, when she finally owns up to disliking asparagus. "I wonder whether my feelings about asparagus are not emblematic of the way in which I have lived much of my life; not acknowledging my preferences or standing up for what I wanted, for instance. Pretending. Acting as if I found people's behavior acceptable when I did not: People said or did things I found hurtful and I would rarely speak up. *I was deaf to the voice inside trying to guide me. Or if I heard it, I ignored it"* (bold italics mine).

And to press the point, the divine law of synchronicity gave me all the information I needed to validate my new creative insight about self-honesty and intuition; Schwartz continues: "I believe most of us know in our hearts, when we are uncomfortable in our skins or unhappy in our jobs or when we do not feel sheltered in our own homes. We know when a relationship isn't working or a friendship has run its course. But we are often reluctant to own up to what we know, even to ourselves, because then we might have to do something about it. Inertia is a powerful force. We have heard the rationale about the devil you know being preferable to the one you don't; many of us choose the path of least resistance—*even as our inner voice encourages us to deviate from it"* (bold italics mine).

How true! And she brings her confessional thought piece and my creative insight to fitting closure with a personal anecdote of going to a restaurant with friends *that her inner voice had told her not to go to*: "But as I left the restaurant, I thought how an evening that should have been pleasant had left me feeling wrung out and blue. I thought how I wished I had chosen to listen to my own voice, to be truer to myself. Why hadn't I simply bowed out of dinner? I thought how I had spent too long in this life pretending that things were fine when they weren't—and that I liked things when I didn't: things like soul-crushing meals in restaurants. And asparagus."

I put the paper down, smiling once more at the miraculous power of synchronicity; and then I called the archetypal lady seeker back up from the depths of my creative unconscious and shared Susan Schwartz's soul-scouring article with her.

The lady seeker smiled, and contritely responded: "She's right. I don't hear my little voice, because I only hear what I want to hear. So, tell me more about this teaching."

"That," I said, "would be another scenario."

PART FOUR

"Jung often used to say that if our civilization perished it would be due more to stupidity than to evil."

JUNG, HIS LIFE AND WORK
Barbara Hannah

30. The Perennial Philosophy

Aldous Huxley introduced me to the concept of perennial philosophy many years ago with his book *The Perennial Philosophy*, which I quickly devoured, as I did every other book that addressed my need to understand the Way that I had awakened to with Gurdjieff's teaching and the sayings of Jesus; but when I read what Ken Wilber had to say about the perennial philosophy in his book *Grace and Grit,* the remarkable love story of his five year marriage to Treya Killam who died of cancer, I was called to do a spiritual musing on the perennial philosophy because I saw that Wilber was talking about the perennial philosophy from the outside (exoteric), as the great intellectual synthesizer of spiritual knowledge that constitutes the perennial philosophy, while I understood the perennial philosophy from the inside (esoteric) as an initiate of the Way; and I was tapped on my shoulder to do a spiritual musing on the distinction between our two perspectives—just as I had done with my musing "A Cheap Shot at Shirley MacLaine" on our different perspectives on reincarnation...

Ken Wilber was an early bloomer. He wrote his exceptionally brilliant book *The Spectrum of Consciousness* when he was only twenty-three years old, which reminded me of British author Colin Wilson, another brilliant early bloomer who wrote *The Outsider* at twenty-four that launched his writing career (and also tainted him for life); but when I took a break from reading *Grace and Grit* yesterday afternoon in the cool, refreshing shade of the maple tree in our front yard to have an after-work drink with Penny, I couldn't help but compare my own journey through life with Ken Wilber's—

"I can't get over Wilber writing *The Spectrum of Consciousness* when he was only twenty-three years old," I shared with Penny, and took a stiff sip of brandy on the rocks which I felt I needed (*Grace and Grit* hit my emotional center hard). "It's not like he was free to write it," I reflected, overwhelmed by his precocious accomplishment. "He took some time off his master's degree at the time and was washing dishes in a restaurant when he wrote it; and he must have read two or three hundred books for his research—*God!*"

"He must be an old soul," Penny replied, with a nod of indifference.

"Even so, he was an early bloomer," I responded, unable to get over his phenomenal accomplishment. "He said that when he wrote the first two paragraphs of *The Spectrum of Consciousness* he knew that's what he wanted to do for the rest of his life. 'I'm home,' he said. He had found his path in writing. God; I wish I would've had that kind of discipline in my youth. But it wouldn't have happened anyway."

"Why not?" Penny asked.

"Because I'm a late bloomer. Besides, you need exceptionally good soil to bloom at such an early age. My family consciousness wasn't conducive to that kind of growth; but I don't want to go there. I don't want to upset myself—"

All of my life I felt like I was trying to catch up to myself, like I had to run the race just to get to the starting line; but not Ken Wilber. He caught up to himself so early in life that he bloomed in what he was meant to become at such an early age that his early writing shines with the wisdom of old age—like his mature self had taken up residence in his youthful self and the two became one astonishingly brilliant self; and once I got over my initial resentment of his intimidating precocity I enjoyed reading my two new Ken Wilber books—*The Spectrum of Consciousness* and *Grace and Grit*.

Aldous Huxley defines the perennial philosophy as "the metaphysic that recognizes a divine Reality substantial to the world of things and lives and minds; the philosophy that finds in the soul something similar to, or even identical with, divine Reality; the ethic that places man's final end in the knowledge of the immanent and transcendent Ground of all being." This is the philosophy of the mystic, says Huxley, who drew from the writings of various wisdom traditions and synthesized into one perspective which he called "the perennial philosophy," a term that he appropriated from the philosopher Leibnitz.

And Ken Wilber echoes Huxley: "The perennial philosophy is the worldview that has been embraced by the vast majority of the world's greatest spiritual teachers, philosophers, thinkers, and even scientists. It's called 'perennial' or 'universal' because it shows up in virtually all cultures across the globe and across the ages. We find it in India, Mexico, China, Japan, Mesopotamia, Egypt, Tibet, Germany, Greece…" (*Grace and Grit,* p. 79)

This is the outer, exoteric perspective on the perennial philosophy; a glimpse at what this "metaphysic" is and which I *know* to be the Way. But just what is this universal metaphysical worldview that has been embraced by all wisdom traditions?

Huxley identified it as the "Ground of all being," which he called "divine Reality," and which all mystics recognize as the Way—the path back home to God; but as the Sufi wisdom tradition has come to realize that every soul is its own path to God because every soul has its own karmic relationship with life, the Way (the universal path home to God) is individualized by every soul—which is why St. Padre Pio told me in one of my spiritual healing sessions for my novel *Healing with Padre Pio* that **"life is a journey of the self."** And the Neo-Platonist philosopher Plotinus confirms this view with his comment that our journey home to God is a flight of the alone to the Alone.

In effect, the Way is an individual path that has to be worked out according to one's own karmic need for spiritual growth. And because not everyone has the same need for spiritual growth, we all have our own relative understanding of the Way.

In *The Power of Flow, Practical Ways to Transform Your Life with Meaningful Coincidence,* authors Charlene Belitz and Meg Lundstrom relate Texas attorney Dan Muse's relative understanding of the Way. Dan says that his purpose in life is "to grow, to have a more profound understanding of life's cycle. And hopefully to be involved in an effort to advance us beyond what we are now." (*The Power of Flow,* p. 56)

The Power of Flow all but defines the mysterious power of synchronicity as the omniscient guiding light of the Way, but when I awakened to the Way as I "worked" on myself with Gurdjieff's teaching and the sayings of Jesus I saw the Way everywhere as the inherently self-transcending power of Holy Spirit—the Voice of God calling us home; and the more I *lived* the Way (i.e., I listened to the Voice of God when it spoke to me through signs, symbols, and coincidences), the more conscious I became of the Way, until I became so conscious of the Way that I simply *knew* that the Way just IS!

In effect, I had awakened to the metaphysical fact that the divine Ground of all being is Holy Spirit, and that Holy Spirit is the Way; ergo, the Way just IS. This is why the Way can be found in all wisdom traditions of the world and called the perennial philosophy.

But not only can it be found in all wisdom traditions, it can be found in every aspect of life—because the Way *is* life; and waking up to the Way is waking up to life. And vice versa: the more we wake up to how life works, the more we wake up to the Way. This is why St. Padre Pio told me that ***"life is all about growth and understanding,"*** and that I should live my life first and only then write about it; sage advice, which I took to heart.

I should have known this, though; because this is what my literary mentor Ernest Hemingway did. He lived his life with passionate intensity and then wrote about it in his stories, like *The Old Man and the Sea* which garnered him the Nobel Prize for literature. This is why he said to me in a dream one night when I was in my early twenties and living in the beautiful Alpine city of Annecy, France, "I have pissed out more life than you have lived," which was the great writer's way of telling me that I had to grow in my understanding of life before I could write about it with authenticity. That's why he wrote in *A Moveable Feast,* the poignantly melancholic memoir of his youthful apprenticeship days in Paris, France, that he began every story he wrote with one true sentence. "Do not worry. You have always written before and you will write now. All you have to do is write one true sentence. Write the truest sentence that you know," he counseled himself.

Hemingway's stories ring true because they are fraught with the consciousness of his lust for life. He loved fishing, hunting, drinking, boxing, and having extra-marital sex; and to write with authenticity I had to find my own way in life, which I did with Gurdjieff's teaching of "work on oneself." And as I lived life my way with no less passionate intensity than Hemingway lived life his way, I became increasingly more conscious of life until I awakened to the

Way, otherwise known to the world as the perennial philosophy; so thanks to Ernest Hemingway, whom I discovered in my tender youth in high school, whenever I write something new today I can proudly say that I begin with the truest sentence that I know, which always springs from my gnostic awareness that the Way just IS. This is how I gave birth to my personal motto: ***life is an individual journey…***

31. Our Sacred Contract

"Because I can no longer ignore death, I pay more attention to life," said Treya (Terry) Killam Wilber in Ken Wilber's book *Grace and Grit,* the remarkable story of their spiritual journey through Treya's five year ordeal with cancer which ended on a joyfully tragic note that transcended the stark reality of her physical death; but no sooner did I finish reading their story of love and suffering and I knew intuitively that this was the sacred contract that they had obligated themselves to fulfill in this life.

As much as I was hoping that Treya would find a cure for her breast cancer which spread throughout her body, I knew upon completing the book that she was not meant to be cured; because it was her sacred contract to die a **conscious death** so she could share it with the world, which she did in her journals that her writer husband wove seamlessly into the story of their inspiring life together. In fact, Ken got his title *Grace and Grit* from the last journal entry that Treya made when she finally surrendered her life to God—

"I got her journal," said Ken, "and a pen, and in clear bold words she wrote" 'It takes grace, yes—and grit!'" And in surrendering to her destined purpose, she experienced the rapturous joy of fulfilling her sacred contract: "I put Treya in bed that evening, and sat down next to her. She had become almost ecstatic. 'I'm going. I can't believe it, I'm going. I'm so happy, I'm so happy, I'm so happy.' Like a mantra of final release, she kept repeating, 'I'm so happy, I'm so happy…'" (*Grace and Grit,* pp. 390-1)

What a relief to leave this world knowing that you have lived up to the responsibility of your sacred contract with the dignity and courage of grace and grit, which is why I was so fearful when I had open heart surgery four years ago because I had not yet realized my life's purpose and would possibly leave this world unfulfilled once more; but I did not know that I had a "sacred contract" until I read Caroline Myss's book *Sacred Contracts*, which, by a happy coincidence that I can only attribute to providential design, I had just read prior to reading *Grace and Grit*—yet one more reason to believe that our life is choreographed!

But whether we call it a sacred contract or our life's purpose, it's the karmic obligation that we owe to ourselves; and we have a sacred duty to honor it so we can continue on our journey home to God where we came from.

This whole business of sacred contracts is still very much up in the air, though; and in order to do it justice I have to call upon my Muse and do a spiritual musing on it...

The theme of Caroline Myss's book *Sacred Contracts* is all about waking up to our life's mission; but not all of us are blind to our life's mission. Some of us come into this world knowing what we have to do, because we are "called" to our life's purpose. This is why Ken Wilber said "I'm home" when he wrote the first two paragraphs of his first book *The Spectrum of Consciousness*; because he *knew* that he was born to be a writer.

I've always had the strangest feeling growing up that "I am the last of my own line," as I expressed it, which explained why I never had the desire to have children; but I had absolutely no idea what this strange feeling meant until I discovered reincarnation.

It took a few years, but I finally realized that this strange feeling that I had growing up that I was the last of my own line was my sacred contract pushing at the door of my consciousness mind, my sacred contract with myself to break my cycle of karma and reincarnation; and in so doing I would be the last of my own line.

This was my calling, then; my mission, or life's purpose. This is why I became a seeker at such an early age. I was born to find the Way so I could break my cycle of karma and reincarnation and complete my spiritual journey to my true self; but there was a clause in my sacred contract that obligated me to share my story with the world—just as there was a clause in Treya's sacred contract to share her experience of dying consciously with the world, which she did by keeping a detailed journal of her cancer ordeal.

This brings to mind Marion Woodman, the Jungian therapist from London, Ontario who also kept a journal of her cancer ordeal, which was also diagnosed "terminal" by her doctors. Unlike Treya however, Marion didn't die; and she shared her cancer ordeal and miraculous healing in her book *Bone, A Journal of Wisdom, Strength, and Healing.*

"This book is about living, not dying," she wrote in the *Forward.* "It's about dying into life. With cancer I discovered how much dying it takes to get here, here into my body, here onto Earth. It's about the soul work required to heal both."

Obviously (at least to me) Marion Woodman's sacred contract was to heal herself of "terminal" cancer so she could share her incredible story of "dying into life" with the world; but as miraculous as her courageous cancer ordeal was, she still could not quite grasp the implication of her "dying into life" insight. She writes in the *Forward* of her book:

"At least initially cancer presented itself to me as a way of dying rather than a way of living. Life and death were the opposites of each other, the one excluding the other. Only gradually did I realize how intimately connected they are, the one existing not in the absence but in the presence of the other. Death present in cancer was death asking to be accepted into my life. Living with cancer as a 'dying into life' still remains a way of living that I do not yet fully understand…"

My first published novel was inspired by a woman who was also dying of cancer. Ruth Picardie was given one year to live, and she decided to write a book (*Before I Say Goodbye*) to tell her family and friends all the things that she felt she should have said but didn't. In a sudden burst of synoptic insight, the soul of my novel announced itself to me and *What Would I Say Today If I Were to Die Tomorrow?* was born!

I put myself under the sword of Damocles, and for six weeks I lived with the threat of death hanging over my head. True, my death threat was imaginary; nonetheless, I lived *as though* tomorrow was going to be my last day on earth, and this gave all the license I needed to get everything that I wanted to say off my chest—which I did, to the horror of my family, friends, and hometown. That's why Penny and I had to relocate to Georgian Bay; but that's another story, which I may work into a novel one day. (The soul of this novel has already announced itself: *We May Be Tiny, But We're Not Small*; which is a play upon where we live in Georgian Bay, the county of Tiny Township.)

Now, just what exactly does it mean to have a sacred contract? Can we know definitively that we all come into the world with a sacred contract?

Doctor Michael Newton, the editor of the book *Memories of the Afterlife*, has done extensive research on the subject of past lives. He authored two books on past lives, *Destiny of Souls,* and *Journey of Souls*; and in *Memories of the Afterlife* which he oversaw and edited Trish Casimira, a hypnotherapist who trained with Doctor Newton and specializes in regression therapy, wrote in Chapter Eight, "A Shattered Heart": "People often seek past-life regression to understand the pattern of why their relationships go bad. Life-between-lives regression reveals that relationships with members in our soul group fulfill a **contract** that was agreed to prior to incarnation. At birth, we agree to forget that arrangement so that we can have the experience without any influence of memory. Even so, amnesic blocks can be removed through hypnotic regression" (p.77).

Doctor Newton's research indicates that we all come into the world with a sacred contract; a karmic need for reconciliation, growth and development, or whatever, and it is our sacred obligation to find our life's mission and honor our contract. But if we don't know what our purpose in life is, we feel cast adrift and lost; which is probably why the Greek philosopher Socrates concluded that the unexamined life was not worth living.

Happy is he then who knows what he wants out of life. But knowing what you want out of life doesn't necessarily mean that you're going to get it. And if there is one thing that I have learned about honoring our sacred contract, it is this: **you have to be true to yourself to live your own life; otherwise you're only deceiving yourself.**

As the mystic Sufi poet Rumi said, "Don't be satisfied with stories, how things have gone with others. Unfold your own myth…"

32. A Window on the Soul of Man

Poets are blessed with the special gift of sight; a sixth sense that allows them to see what the rest of us cannot see. But even though we cannot see what they see, we feel the truth of what they see; this is why we love poetry. It's a window on the soul of man.

For the past few weeks I've been strongly nudged (to the point of irritation) to write a spiritual musing on the soul of man, which I think started with my research into Ken Wilber's panoramic philosophy of life. I just finished reading *Grace and Grit*, the five year breast cancer ordeal that he saw his wife through; a profoundly moving story of love and suffering, courage, and passionate equanimity; a beautiful, beautiful story. But it stirred something in me—a very strong desire to deal with the question of the soul of man.

I tried to put it off, but it wouldn't go away; it kept buzzing around in my mind like a pesky little fly that refused to go away, and everything I read seemed to fuel the desire to write a spiritual musing on the soul of man, especially Andrew Cohen's best-selling "cutting edge" book *Evolutionary Enlightenment* that combusted the fire of my desire.

And believe me, I tried half a dozen times to find an entry point, but I just couldn't find my way into my musing on the soul of man; until this morning, that is.

For some reason known only to the omniscient guiding force of life, the romantic poet John Keats popped into my mind, and I knew instantly that he was my point of entry; so I looked up the letter that he wrote to his brother called "The Vale of Soul Making," and when I read the phrase "atoms of perception," which was his description of the embryonic soul of man, I was given the green light for today's spiritual musing…

But why was my Muse so insistent that I muse upon the soul of man? I had never been nudged so strongly to write a spiritual musing ever since I began writing them for my first volume of spiritual musings *Just Going With the Flow*; what was it about the soul of man that my Muse wanted me to bring to the fore—because that's the essential purpose of my creative self-reflections, to make conscious the unconscious nature of man's soul?

What really threw fuel onto the fire of my desire to write today's musing was the entire premise of Andrew Cohen's (and Buddhism's) philosophical perspective, which he asserts throughout his whole book *Evolutionary Enlightenment* (and which is implicit to Wilber's *Grace and Grit*) and can be summed up in the following synoptic passage:

"From the perspective of the rational mind, a human life is a linear, limited event, circumscribed by the inescapable march of time from birth to death. But when you penetrate beyond the mind, you directly see, know, and feel that instead of merely being an individual body, mind, and personality that was born and is going to die, you are that empty ground of Being that has never become anything.

"That primordial ground is who you *always* are, no matter how things may appear at any given moment in time; it is the very essence of your own self at its most fundamental level. How can you know that? Because, as we have discovered, when every attribute that you habitually identify as being *you* falls away, your deepest sense of self is still there. But that self has no name, no history, no gender, no personal identity. It is not really *your* self—it is *the* Self, the absolute subject. It is singular. Consciousness is the primordial state of the "I" of the entire cosmos—the subjectivity or interiority of everything that exists." (Andrew Cohen, *Evolutionary Enlightenment*, p. 17)

In a word, Cohen is echoing the Buddhist philosophy that we have no self, as such; that the personal self we think we have is merely a stream of consciousness that draws its identity from mental concepts and memories, all of which are impermanent, and when our body dies so does our illusory sense of personal self. But every fiber of my being shouts NO to this perspective, and my Muse will not rest easy until we set the record straight.

This is hard, though. To set the record straight I have to go against twenty-five centuries of Buddhist thought; and I keep asking myself, could they have gotten it wrong all these years? *But they didn't get it wrong!* I know this. They are right when they say that we have only one Self, that this Ground of all Being is who we are—the "I" of Consciousness; I know this is true, because I experienced the Oneness of the Universe, I experienced the "I" of God—*but I also experienced the "I" of my own individual Soul self!*

How can this be? How can I have an individual Soul self, an "I" distinct but not separate from the "I" of the one Self of Consciousness and Ground of all Being? This is why I resisted writing today's spiritual musing, because my perspective—which was born of my experience of giving birth to my spiritual self—goes so far beyond the popular current of the today's "cutting edge" thought on the evolution of consciousness that it would jar the whole non-self paradigm and upset the Buddhist applecart.

Thank God for the poets, then; because they have caught a glimpse of what I have experienced. Rumi, the most mystical of poets, saw the distinction between the illusory self of our bodily personality and the individuated Soul self of our spiritual evolution through life: **"These leaves, our bodily personalities, seem identical,/ but the globe of soul fruit/we make,/each is elaborately/unique"** (Bill Moyers, *The Language of Life, A Festival of Poets*, p. 48); and John Keats, whose letter "The Vale of Soul Making" penetrates the veil of life and goes straight to heart of the Divine Plan of God:

"There may be intelligences or sparks of divinity in millions, but they are not Souls until they acquire identities, till each one is personally itself. Intelligences are atoms of perception—they know and they see and they are pure; in short, they are God. How then are Souls to be made? How then are these sparks which are God to have identity given them—so as even to possess a bliss peculiar to each one by individual existence? How but by the medium of a world like this?" (*Values*, by J. G. Bennett, p. 12)

John Keats caught a glimpse of our spiritual purpose in life, which is to create our own self-identity—"a bliss peculiar to each one by individual existence," or a "globe of soul fruit" as Rumi expressed it. This is not what Ken Wilber, Andrew Cohen, and the Buddhist tradition maintain, though; they believe that this individual identity is illusory, a transient self that passes through life into nothingness; they believe that this miraculous "bliss" of God is a non-self that is not what it is. They believe that our personal self is an illusion.

Why life, then? Why "the medium of a school like this?" Or, as the Preacher in the *Book of Ecclesiastes* expressed it, "What profit hath a man of all his labor which he taketh under the sun?" Why would God bother with the world, with life, with the whole evolutionary process of *being* and *becoming* if not to give birth to itself through each of its pure un-self-realized atoms of perception and recreate its own identity and experience its own "bliss," its own God self through each and every spark of its divine nature?

This is the mystery I was born to resolve. This was my sacred contract. And this is why I was terrified of writing this spiritual musing, because who would believe me if I told them that during one of my seven past-life regressions I experienced myself as an atom of God in the Body of God? That I had Soul consciousness but no self-consciousness, and that I was sent into these lower worlds to evolve through the evolutionary process of life to acquire my own individual self-identity? That after millions of incarnations through countless life forms I finally experienced the birth of my own reflective self-consciousness in my lifetime as a higher primate? And that I continued to evolve in self-realization consciousness through the natural process of karma and reincarnation until in my current lifetime I was self-realized enough to take evolution into my own hands with the secret teachings of the Way and gave birth to my spiritual self in my mother's kitchen one day while she was kneading bread dough on the kitchen table? That I broke the cycle of karma and reincarnation and transcended myself and could say, **"I am what I am not, and I am not what I am; I am both, but neither: I am Soul."** Who would believe this?

But does it really matter? The point of this spiritual musing is to offer a perspective that will expand the view on the soul of man, a view that does not deny the validity of the Buddhist perspective (because it is valid also, but it is only one half of the story of the soul of man); and the only way I can do this is to tell the story of how I came to realize the bliss of my own spiritually self-realized consciousness, which I do with every book that I write because this is also part of my sacred contract.

33. The Omniscient Guiding Force And Vicissitudes of Life

A few days before his death, the psychologist Carl Jung was asked by an interviewer for *Good Housekeeping Magazine* (Dec. 1961) about his notion of God. To the interviewer's surprise, he replied in these words: "To this day God is the name by which I designate all things which cross my willful path violently and recklessly, all things which upset my subjective views, plans and intentions and change the course of my life for better or worse." (*Ego and Archetype,* by Edward F. Edinger, p. 101)

In this context Jung is calling God what most people call chance or accident. For Jung, everything in life is saturated with psychic meaning; this is why he held the view that all the vicissitudes of the outer and inner life have a meaning and are expressions of transpersonal patterns and powers. Ralph Waldo Emerson held the same view. He said: "The secret of the world is the tie between person and event…the soul contains the event that shall befall it. Events grow on the same stem with persons."

From this perspective, there are no accidents; everything in life is related and meaningful. This is a powerful insight, and today's spiritual musing…

There seems to be a voracious need in the world today, especially in western society, to find meaning in one's life (as expressed in the many books and little cottage industries on how to live the authentic life), as though the natural connection that we have with life has been severed—if we do have a natural connection with life, that is; otherwise, as the existentialist Jean Paul Sartre believed, our life is contingent, meaningless, and absurd.

"Man is a useless passion," said Sartre; but what if man has a natural connection with life that speaks to an inherent teleological purpose? In *Memories, Dreams, Reflections* Jung says: "The decisive question for man is: Is he related to something infinite or not?" And in *Ecclesiastes* the Preacher asks the question: "What profit hath a man of all his labor which he taketh under the sun?" This sums up the Sartrean and Jungian quandary very nicely.

So, are we related to something infinite or not? Because if we are, then what would this relationship be? Sartre can't help us. He has abandoned all hope and condemns man to the freedom that he posits with the choices he makes. "Man is condemned to be free," said the atheist philosopher; but Jung, who believed in God, came to believe that God needs man to illuminate the consciousness of God through human experience.

For the atheist philosopher man is not related to something infinite. Man is born, lives, and dies; end of story. For the psychologist who believed in God, man is related to something infinite; and his purpose in life is to expand the consciousness of God through the individuation of that spark of divine consciousness that he called the Archetypal Self.

Jung would answer the Preacher this way, then: the purpose of all of man's labor under the sun is to individuate the Archetypal Self. Like the ancient alchemists before him, Jung believed that man must finish the work which nature left incomplete; and he devoted his life to making conscious the natural process of individuation that evolves man to the point where he has to take evolution into his own hands to realize his teleological purpose.

"Unconscious wholeness therefore seems to me the true *spiritus rector* of all biological and psychic events," wrote Jung. "Here is a principle which strives for total realization—which in man's case signifies the attainment of total consciousness. Attainment of consciousness in culture in the broadest sense, and self-knowledge is therefore the heart and essence of the process." (*Memories, Dreams, Reflections*, p. 324-5)

Late in his life, just before his death, Jung had the following dream. He saw "high up in a high place" a boulder lit by the full sun. Carved into the illuminated boulder were the words: "Take this as a sign of the wholeness of self you have achieved and the singleness you have become." (*Our Dreaming Mind,* Robert L. Van de Castle Ph.D., p. 145)

Jung believed that the path leading to self-realization and personal wholeness could be achieved, and his dream confirmed it; but, as he told Miguel Serrano, "the path is very hard." Which is why

Jesus said *"many are called but few are chosen."* Two questions arise here: 1, What is the path? And 2, Why is the path so hard?

Jesus tells us that he *is* the path. *"I am the way, the truth, and the life,"* he said; but he added, *"no man cometh unto the Father but by me."* The whole myth of Christianity rests upon these words, leading the world to believe that only through Jesus Christ can we enter the kingdom of heaven; but Jung believed that the underlying meaning of Christianity is the quest for individuation, which is a personal responsibility.

When Gurdjieff said that nature will only evolve us so far and no further, he was echoing the alchemist teaching that we must complete what nature left unfinished; and what did nature leave unfinished? The process of individuation; that's what!

Nature cannot individuate the consciousness of the Archetypal Self to wholeness and singleness of self; we have to do that ourselves. And we do that by taking evolution into our own hands by putting our hand to the plow, as Jesus said. This is his metaphor for stepping upon the path to wholeness and singleness of self.

I stepped upon the path when I took up Gurdjieff's teaching of "work on oneself." And the more I "worked" on myself, the more I awakened to the Way; which I soon found in the sayings of Jesus. And after years of "working" on myself I gave birth to my spiritual self in my mother's kitchen while she was kneading bread dough on the kitchen table; so I know what the path is, and that when *lived* it will complete what nature left unfinished.

When I awakened to the Way I realized something about the Way that everyone who awakens to the Way will realize—that the Way is Divine Spirit, which is the omniscient guiding force and divine energy responsible for all life. I realized that the Way *is* life, and that we *are* the Way; but we are not awake to the Way until we be begin to live the Way consciously. And we live the Way consciously by making concerted efforts to "work" on ourselves with the teachings of the Way provided for us by teachers of the Way, such as Jesus, Gurdjieff, and C. G. Jung to name only three; this is why the path is very hard.

We are never alone, then; because the Way is always with us in the *process of life* itself. This puts a whole new light on the many vicissitudes of life, because all the twists and turns and ups and downs that we have to go through in life are expressions of our own individuation process. These vicissitudes are *our* own Way, if you will; *our* own individual path to wholeness and singleness of self—whether we are conscious of it or not.

This is why when Jung was asked what his notion of God was he replied: "God is the name by which I designate all things which cross my willful path violently and recklessly, all things which upset my subjective views, plans and intentions and change the course of my life for better or worse." Jung found God in ***the process of life***, and he gave us his psychology of individuation to help us complete what nature left unfinished.

34. Stupidity Is Not a Gift of God

*"What one has done in the secret chamber,
one has someday to cry aloud on the housetops."*

De Profundis, Oscar Wilde

I just finished reading a new book on the shadow self, the repressed side of our personality, called *The Shadow Effect*, by three well-known authors: Deepak Chopra, Debbie Ford, and Marianne Williamson; and as illuminating as it was, it only confirmed what I had painfully come to realize in my own quest for authenticity.

A great deal of attention today is being focused on the authentic self, and every "life coach" has his/her own theory on how to be your authentic self—from Dr. Wayne Dyer to Gary Zukav to Carolyn Myss and company—but is the path to authenticity such a mystery that it takes the collective genius of all these authors to point the way for us?

The short answer is YES. And this in itself is a great mystery, because the path to authenticity is only visible to those that have, as Jesus expressed it, "eyes to see and ears to hear," and unless we are ready to awaken to the path to authenticity we will never recognize it. *But wait!* God is merciful. We are not alone in our plight. Built into the evolutionary process of life is the inherently self-correcting law of the individuation process; and as painful as this corrective law of life may be, it is our saving grace.

Today's "life coaches" all have their own understanding of this mysterious law, and each one renders it into their own personal path to authenticity (and in the process start yet another cottage industry, each one striving to rival the "Chicken Soup for the Soul" phenomenon); but just what this unseen law of inherent self-transcendence is, they cannot tell us because they can't seem to pin it down. Each one catches a glimpse of this divine law, but no-one has seen its face. This, then, is the challenge of today's spiritual musing…

STUPIDITY IS NOT A GIFT OF GOD

"The conflict between who we are and who we want to be is at the core of the human struggle," writes Debbie Ford in the introduction to *The Shadow Effect*; and she and her colleagues Deepak Chopra and Marianne Williamson go on to explain that the shadow is responsible for this conflict; and although they offer us a wonderful insight into the psyche of man, they fail to explain the reason why we are in conflict in the first place.

Debbie Ford gives a clear description of her and her colleagues' path to authenticity in the following statement: "Our shadow incites us to act out in ways we never imagined we could and to waste our vital energy on bad habits and repetitive behaviors. Our shadow keeps us from full self-expression, from speaking our truth, and from living an authentic life. It is only by embracing our duality that we free ourselves of the behaviors that can potentially bring us down. If we don't acknowledge all of who we are, we are guaranteed to be blindsided by the shadow effect." (*The Shadow Effect*, p. 2)

To our complete dismay, we sabotage our own success in life when we make a choice in a haze of unconsciousness that undermines the progress we've worked years to realize; this is what Ford and her colleagues mean by the ***shadow effect.*** As humorous as it may sound, our shadow pops out of the deep recesses of our psyche to sabotage our conscious life; which is precisely what I explored in my book *Old Whore Life, Exploring the Shadow Side of Karma* and what I further explored in this third volume of spiritual musings.

The ***shadow effect*** catches a glimpse of the self-correcting law of the individuation process. Debbie Ford writes: "All self-sabotage is an externalization of the internal shame hidden in the dark recesses of our unconscious minds. Because we have not had the wisdom, courage, or wherewithal to make peace with what we have suppressed out of guilt, fear, or shame, it gets forced into the open so that we can reclaim and embrace our lost self and return to the transparent state of our whole self." (*The Shadow Effect*, p. 114)

Briefly stated, the authentic self corrects its own behavior by the very nature of the evolutionary impulse to individuate which, as Jung realized, strives for total consciousness; so when we sabotage our conscious life by blindly obstructing our own individuation process, it is nature's way of telling us that we have to align our outer life with our inner life. In other words, there is something about our life that is out of sync with the natural flow of the life process; and the *shadow effect* is one way that the inherent law of self-transcendence comes to our aid. So, just what is this law of inherent self-transcendence that kicks in with the devastating, self-destructive *shadow effect*?

The answer lies in our two destinies. But to make sense of what I mean by our two destines I have to posit my own perspective on the evolutionary impulse to individuate, which was born of my conscious efforts to realize my true self and my seven past-life regressions that gave me an insight into the Divine Plan of God.

Having worked out from my past-life regressions that we all come from the Body of God as un-self-realized atoms of God planted in these lower worlds to evolve in consciousness until we realize our divine nature through the natural impulse to individuate the consciousness of God, I came to the realization as I lived the individuation process with conscious intent (beginning with Gurdjieff's system of "work on oneself" and Christ's teaching of spiritual rebirth) that we are all teleologically driven to realize our divine nature, which is our spiritual destiny; but **our spiritual destiny can only be realized within the parameters of our personal karmic destiny, which is determined from life to life by the choices we make.** Hence, we have a predetermined spiritual destiny that we are all born to realize, and from which we cannot escape, and a personal karmic destiny which we determine by the choices we make; and our purpose in life is to align our two destinies.

As I learned from my past-life regressions, it takes many lifetimes to come to the realization that we have two destinies; in fact, it takes many lifetimes to realize that we are the authors of our own karmic destiny. For example, I had a past lifetime in Paris, France in the mid 17th Century that was sexually debauched and morally depraved. I enslaved women sexually and took immeasurable pleasure in depraving them; but in my next lifetime I was born as a black slave in southern Georgian, USA.

I incurred a karmic debt with life in my debauched Parisian lifetime, and I had to pay life back for sexually enslaving all those women; and I began to pay my debt by being born into a life of slavery, which was one of the most painful lives I ever lived. I died in that lifetime wondering why God would condemn me to a life of slavery, and I did not realize until my current lifetime why I had destined myself to a life of slavery and suffering.

As I gradually pieced together the Divine Plan of God, I began to see that suffering was nature's way of burning off karma, which is reflected in the Christian belief that "suffering is good for the soul." But this only makes sense within the context of our spiritual and karmic destinies; otherwise suffering boggles the human mind. *But how much must we suffer before we learn that we are the authors of our own karmic destiny?*

This is how the realization that stupidity is not a gift of God was forced upon me, because it is entirely man-made by the choices we make, whether we make these choices consciously or unconsciously. Like the cartoon figure of a man who gets electrocuted by trying to splice a wire that is live with electric current. He can't blame God for getting shocked by the electric current, because he should have known better. But what if he didn't know any better, as I didn't know that I would condemn myself to a future life of slavery by living such a debauched lifetime in Paris, France? Is that fair?

It is neither fair nor unfair, because karma is impersonal. Karma is nature's merciful law of just compensation, and it will do whatever it can to keep life in a state of balance; and if our personal life is out of balance with life's natural impulse to individuate the consciousness of God (our spiritual destiny), then the corrective law of life kicks in to bring our karmic destiny into agreement with our spiritual destiny, and by corrective law of life I mean Divine Spirit, or what I have come to call the omniscient guiding force of life.

Synchronicities, or meaningful coincidences, are one way that the omniscient guiding force of life brings our outer and inner life to a ***choice point*** where we can align our karmic destiny with our spiritual destiny because we are out of sync with life.

This is the theme of my novel *Tea with Grace, A Story of Synchronicity and Platonic Love.* Grace Kendal's spiritual destiny has become hampered by her Roman Catholic faith, and the merciful law of synchronicity provides a ***choice point*** for her to reconcile her outer life with her inner life; but because it is her choice, she can heed the Call of Soul or not heed it, and with dramatic tension *Tea with Grace* illustrates what Debbie Ford meant when she said, "The conflict between who we are and who we want to be is at the core of the human struggle," Grace Kendal could not become who she wanted to be (her spiritual destiny), because her Christian faith inhibited her spiritual growth; hence her conflict.

Like Grace Kendal, I could not become who I wanted to be because my spiritual destiny was inhibited by the path I had chosen to live. I had taken the path of business (I had a pool hall and vending machine business in my early twenties), but the omniscient guiding force of life saw that this path would inhibit my spiritual destiny, and I had a sexual experience one night that shocked my conscience awake and catapulted me into my spiritual quest for my true self; *but it took many years to come to the realization that my outer life had been sabotaged by my repressed shadow self with that shocking sexual experience!*

Our shadow self is not limited to our current-life personality, because we create a new shadow self with each life we live; and when we die, our personality (which includes our repressed shadow) does not fade away into oblivion; we take it with us in our Soul body. And when we are reborn into our next life our former personality and shadow come with us as our unconscious self, which is teleological driven to individuate the consciousness of God; and when I had that sexual experience that shocked my conscience awake I came to realize many years later that it was my sexually debauched Parisian personality that came out of the deep recesses of my unconscious to possess me to do what I did, and out of shame and guilt I had to sell my business and go on a quest for my true self because I knew in my heart that it wasn't me who did what I did that night. It was me, but not me; and it took years to come to the realization that it was my deeply repressed, unresolved shadow self.

Despite the fact that we may not be conscious of the Spiritual Law of Karma, we are nonetheless determined by it by the choices we make; and we cannot blame God for our suffering, because we bring it upon ourselves by the inherently corrective law of life. And if we persist in creating karma that destines us to more suffering, we will just keep coming back until we wake up to the fact that we are the authors of our own destiny. As the saying goes, we will just keep coming back until we get it right; and getting it right is learning how to bring our outer life into agreement with our inner life—because, as Debbie Ford said, "If we don't acknowledge all of who we are, we are guaranteed to be blindsided by the shadow effect." *That's why stupidity is not a gift of God!*

35. Life Only Makes Sense When We Know Why We Are Here

"There is nothing but the self and God."
Love without End, Jesus Speaks
Glenda Green

My life changed after I wrote *Healing with Padre Pio*. I did receive a spiritual healing from him that radically transformed my life; or, to be perfectly correct, my experience with St. Padre Pio as I worked on my book (he was channeled by a gifted sensitive for my book) brought me to that place of understanding where a spiritual healing could occur, thereby crediting St. Padre Pio for getting me there and crediting the sanctifying grace of Holy Spirit for my healing, which I'm sure the Good Saint would not disagree with.

My spiritual healing radically transformed my sense of self. I had absolutely no idea that I suffered from spiritual conceit when I went for my healing, and it took the devastating power of the Ascended Master's humility to slay my inflated vanity and precipitate my spiritual healing; but this begs the question: how did I contract the disease of spiritual conceit? This is what I would like to explore in today's spiritual musing…

As with most of my spiritual musings, the idea for this final musing to *Stupidity Is Not a Gift of God* came to me by way of synchronicity. For some reason known only to the omniscient guiding force of life (which in its creative genius is telling me that this musing will bring perfect closure to my book), I was strongly nudged to read yet again (I've read this book two or three times already) *Gurdjieff*, by Louis Pauwels, who was a devout follower of Gurdjieff's transformative teaching of "work on oneself."

In the Forward to *Gurdjieff*, H. L. Dor wrote: "Louis Pauwels was brought to the edge of death by the Gurdjieff exercises. On leaving hospital he decided to see what happened to others. He found that many had been less fortunate, and had in fact died." Which did not really surprise me, because I knew just how hard it was to live Gurdjieff's teaching.

Pauwels' book brings to light how Gurdjieff's teaching radically affected some of his more vulnerable students, and this inspired today's spiritual musing because Gurdjieff's teaching—which came to me by way of a providential coincidence when I was studying philosophy at university—was not only responsible for waking me up to the Way, but for infecting me with the insidious virus of spiritual conceit.

This virus lay dormant for many years, but it was finally activated by the new spiritual teaching that I embraced after I outgrew Gurdjieff's teaching; and it infected my personality to the point where it seriously affected my spiritual growth; hence, the reason for my spiritual healing experience with Ascended Master St. Padre Pio.

So as grateful as I am for Gurdjieff's teaching (I hope to one day lay a yellow rose on his gravesite in Avon, France), had I not awakened to the Way as I "worked" on myself with his teaching I would not have contracted the virus of spiritual conceit; but then, as St. Padre Pio said to me, "You needed that to get here."

I laughed when he told me this. But upon reflection I came to realize that **vanity is a prerequisite for spiritual growth,** and I had a much deeper chuckle at the Humble Saint's incredible sense of irony (*because all spiritual paths consider ego to be our biggest obstacle to spiritual self-realization consciousness!*); but that's material for another musing.

Today I want to explore why I contracted the spiritual virus by waking up to the Way, and how the new spiritual path that I embraced after dropping Gurdjieff's teaching activated the virus that so distorted my sense of self that the divine law of synchronicity had to step in to bring my outer life back into agreement with my inner life, the spiritual path that I have generically referred to in my musings as the Way of the Eternal.

First, then; how did Gurdjieff's teaching of "work on oneself" wake me up to the Way? And just what is the Way, anyway?

Without going into detail on how I came to this realization, which I've done elsewhere in my musings, the Way is the path back home to God, and it is inherent to all paths because the Way is Divine Spirit, which is the essential energy and omniscient guiding force of life. This makes life the Way, because without Divine Spirit there would be no life; and living Gurdjieff's teaching of "work on oneself" woke me up to how the inherently self-transcending power of the Way works in life.

I lived Gurdjieff's teaching in the wilderness, as it were; because I did not know any other person who had even heard of Gurdjieff, let alone lived his teaching. In fact, to this very day more than forty years after discovering Gurdjieff I still have yet to meet another student of his teaching; except in dreams, that is. And I also met Gurdjieff in my dreams throughout the very difficult and formative years of "working" on myself; so I had to be very resourceful and extremely innovative to live his teaching on my own.

I focused on the self-transformative aspects of his teaching, and by this I mean that I learned how to become aware of myself so I could transform the false aspect of my nature and grow in my authentic self. *Self-remembering, non-identification, voluntary effort*, and *consciousness suffering* were the transformative techniques that I employed with pathological commitment every hour of every day; and the more I authenticated my false self, the more awake I became to life. That's how I gravitated to the sayings of Jesus that precipitated my spiritual growth until one day I reached critical mass and shifted my center of gravity from my outer self and realized my inner self.

In a word, I gave birth to my spiritual self. This happened in my mother's kitchen while she was kneading bread dough on the kitchen table; and from that day on I knew I had transcended myself and wrote in my journal: **"I am what I am not, and I am not what I am; I am both, but neither: I am Soul."**

And from this perspective I could *see* the Way. This is why my heart leapt with joy when I read what the founder of my new spiritual path had to say about the Way.

"The Way just IS!" he wrote, and I knew exactly what he meant because I had initiated myself into the mysterious process of how the Way manifested in life; and this validated what Gurdjieff meant when he said that there is only self-initiation into the mysteries of life. And it also confirmed Jung's personal initiation into the mysteries of the Way. He wrote in *The Red Book*: "This life is the way, the long sought-after way to the unfathomable, which we call divine. There is no other way; all other ways are false paths." And it was his initiation into the mysteries of the ***secret way of life*** that inspired Jung to develop his psychology of individuation.

But, ironically, in all these years of living the Way consciously I have yet to meet one other person in my life who can say with categorical certainty that life *is* the Way, or that "the Way just IS." This was the source of my spiritual conceit, along with the very private experience of looking into the Face of God; but it did not infect my personality until I embraced the spiritual path that claims to be "the most direct path to God." With every initiation that I received into a higher order of this secret teaching, the more I grew in my spiritual conceit, and the more inflated I became; but I was oblivious to my own vanity.

And after twenty-five years of living this spiritual teaching I finally received my initiation into the Fifth Plane of Consciousness, which is the Soul Plane and first of the spiritual worlds of God after the Physical, Astral, Causal, and Mental Planes; and the vanity of my spiritual conceit became so inflated with my Fifth Initiation that it was insufferable (to other people, not myself; because I was blind to my own vanity), and I came to a standstill in my spiritual growth.

That's when the merciful law of divine synchronicity stepped in and provided an opportunity (***a choice point***) for a spiritual healing, which inspired my novel *Healing with Padre Pio* and sequel *Why Bother? The Riddle of the Good Samaritan*; and after I wrote these two books I took a break from the outer teachings of this spiritual path, after seriously considering leaving it altogether because my spiritual community is oblivious to its insufferable shadow. So just what does it mean then to *know* that the Way just IS?

The difference between a *gnostic* and *intellectual* awareness of the Way is what activated the virus of spiritual conceit that interrupted the natural impulse to individuate the consciousness of my Soul self, and I stopped growing spiritually; that's why the omniscient guiding force of life arranged for me to meet a spiritual healer who channeled the Ascended Master St. Padre Pio as one of her spiritual guides.

"Life is a journey of the self," said St. Padre Pio, which led me to ask him for validation that we are all born sparks of divine consciousness whose purpose in life is to evolve through the natural process of evolution until we give birth to a new "I" of God and individuate through karma and reincarnation until we are evolved enough to take evolution into our own hands (as I did with Gurdjieff's teaching) until we give birth to our Soul self; and St. Padre Pio, who from his place of all-knowing and all-seeing, agreed with my realization thereby confirming the "Gurdjieff fallacy" that not everyone is born with an immortal soul. We are all born Soul seeds, and we need not fear that when we die we are going to become *"merde,"* as Gurdjieff so crudely put it. "We are all a part of the Whole," the Good Saint answered me; thereby implying that we are all sparks of divine consciousness encoded to become spiritually self-realized and God conscious.

I *realized* that we all come from God as Soul seeds, because in my fourth past-life regression I was brought back to the Body of God where we all originated as Soul seeds; and in the same regression I experienced the birth of my "I" consciousness in my first primordial human lifetime, which challenged the whole Buddhist perspective on the self of man, and I continued to evolve through karma and reincarnation until my current lifetime when I took evolution into my own hands and realized my Soul self. That's why the virus of spiritual conceit bloated me up with so much vanity that I had to have a spiritual healing; and St. Padre Pio, with unbelievable patience and compassion, made me ready for the sanctifying grace of Holy Spirit to come into my life and heal my diseased Soul self.

Life makes sense now because I *know* why we are here. I *know* that we all come from the Body of God as un-self-realized Soul seeds to grow and evolve for the divine purpose of expanding the consciousness of God through the individuation of our Soul self; and we need not despair as so many people are wont to do that life is a "useless passion," because in the grand scheme of things we are as relevant to God as God is to us.

Epilogue

*"There is no other time or place to find yourself.
Now is your only context."*
Love without End, Jesus Speaks
Glenda Green

We all do stupid things, and we hate ourselves for doing them; that's why we repress the memories of our stupidities. But they don't go away just because we have repressed them. They cling together in our unconscious and form an archetypal matrix of psychic energy that can compel us to behave stupidly whenever an opportunity arises, and quite often when we least expect it. This is why I was inspired to write this new book of spiritual musings. I wanted to make conscious this unconscious tendency that we have for doing stupid things; but little did I expect my musings to take me where they did.

C.G. Jung, who has been one of the greatest influences upon my life, said: "My life is a story of the self-realization of the unconscious." So is my life; and so is everyone else's life, because this is the primordial imperative of the life process—we all are forced to become more conscious as we go through life, only some of us try to precipitate the natural process of individuation to satisfy our inherent longing for wholeness.

But even so, we are still subject to moments of stupidity (both great and small), because we cannot help ourselves; and the most that we can do is learn from them. To make my point, one morning we got an email from a friend in Toronto who has a cottage here in Georgian Bay informing us that she would be flying to France for her nephew's wedding, and Penny brought it to my attention that I behaved stupidly when I failed to properly acknowledge the gift of chocolates that our friend had brought back for us from her last holiday in France several years ago; rather than thank her for the box of French chocolates, I informed her that chocolates made me depressed, so I seldom ate chocolates.

Instead of acknowledging her gift with grace (a simple thank you would have sufficed), I nullified it by telling her that chocolate depressed me. Why in God's name would I do that? Couldn't I have chosen a more appropriate time to inform her of how chocolate affected me? What was I thinking?

That's just it, I wasn't thinking; that's why we fall into those little traps that life sets up for us. Life, of course, doesn't actually set traps up for us—which was the theme that I explored in my second volume of spiritual musings, *Old Whore Life, Exploring the Shadow Side of Karma*—because we are the authors of our own circumstances; we just don't have the presence of mind to behave with rational objectivity (let alone sensitivity), and so we are destined to go through life forever learning from our stupid mistakes.

Which is to say that *Stupidity Is Not a Gift of God* was born of the many stupidities of my life, some so small as to be inconsequential, but others so humiliating that they affected my life in ways that would take whole books to unravel; like my experience with an offshoot Christian solar cult teaching that did irreparable damage to my eyesight more than thirty years ago but which I'm still much too embarrassed to write about; but when I brought *Stupidity Is Not a Gift of God* to closure and went through the entire manuscript I was forced to smile at how my Muse had skillfully shifted my creative focus from the dark corners of my own psyche to the shadowy recesses of life in general; for example, "The Gurdjieff Fallacy," "The Fear of Self-knowledge," and especially "The Conversion Experience." These musings dared to focus the light of spiritual awareness on man's inconceivable stupidities, both conscious and unconscious.

After all, who in their right mind would dare call Gurdjieff, the incomparable founder of a comprehensive system of self-transformation that he called the Work, stupid? Certainly not me! His teaching awakened me to the Way, and I will be forever grateful.

But my Muse—well, that's the beauty of letting go and letting Soul speak; it has a mind of its own, and I have learned to trust the creative process.

"As far as we can discern," said Jung in *Memories, Dreams, Reflections,* "the sole purpose of human existence is to kindle a light in the darkness of mere being." I can only hope that *Stupidity Is Not a*

Gift of God has kindled a light in the darkness of our being; because, as Jung went on to say, "It may even be assumed that just as the unconscious affects us, so the increase of our consciousness affects the unconscious."

———♥———

INSIGHTS

A Personal Essay

*On the Evolutionary Impulse to Individuate:
A Response to the Spiritual Path of
Evolutionary Enlightenment*

*"God is not blessed in his Godhead.
He must be born in man forever."*
Meister Eckhart

This essay is my response to the concept "evolutionary enlightenment" that is being advanced by Andrew Cohen, the author of *Evolutionary Enlightenment, A New Path to Spiritual Awakening*. This essay is born of personal experience, and I wish to offer another perspective on this concept that Cohen calls "evolutionary enlightenment."

"Prior to everything, I already am," says Andrew Cohen. "The experience of this recognition is not one of becoming liberated. It is of being *already* liberated." And how one arrives at this realization is the fundamental premise of *Evolutionary Enlightenment;* but how Cohen arrived at this perspective is radically different from how I arrived at it.

Cohen stresses that we don't *become* liberated, we *already* are liberated; but given my experience with the evolutionary process of life, I have to say that Cohen is putting the carriage in front of the horse; and this is the premise of my essay…

An acorn seed is an oak tree *in potentia*; and so are we the Soul seed of our own true divine self. In the simplest terms possible, I have come to realize that to *be* who we are we have to *become* who we are; and from my perspective on the evolutionary impulse to individuate, *becoming* is what the evolutionary process of life is all about.

True, *becoming* presupposes *being*, because how can you *become* without *being*? But it's in how we come to the realization of our own *being* that I wish to illustrate with my own evolutionary experience, which diverges from Cohen's perspective; but where to begin?

I can't help but go back to the poets for my entry point to this essay; Keats in particular, who in a prescient letter to his brother ("The Vale of Soul Making") says "There may be intelligences or sparks of divinity in millions, but they are not Souls till they acquire identities, till each one is personally itself." To *be* we must *become*, says Keats; but how?

He continues: "Intelligences are atoms of perception—they know and they see and they are pure; in short, they are God. How then are Souls to be made? How then are these sparks which are God to have identity given them—so as even to possess a bliss peculiar to each one by individual existence? How but by the medium of a world like this?"

In short, Keats is saying that through life experience we realize our individual identity. Now, at the risk of putting myself way out there I'm going to relate the formative experiences that I had that shed light on Keats's poetic insight into the evolutionary process of Soul's individuation through the "medium of a world like this."

I will start with an experience I had almost forty years ago, which did not make any sense to me at the time. It only made sense when I had seven past-life regressions many years later; only then did I connect all the dots and catch a glaring glimpse of what I came to call the Divine Plan of God, but which I now recognize as **the evolutionary impulse to individuate**. And this evolutionary impulse to individuate is what Keats meant by Souls acquiring an identity, "a bliss peculiar to each one by individual existence."

Why I had this experience was a mystery to me, and it remained a mystery until I had my seven past-life regressions; nonetheless, here is what I experienced: I was sitting in the back yard of our family home in a wind-protected corner just soaking in the spring sun, and it felt so good that I leaned my head back onto the warm stucco of the house and basked.

It had been a long winter as it always is in Northwestern Ontario, and the warm spring sun felt soothing and life-giving. I shut my eyes and took in the sun's rays. I let my mind drift. Gradually, without attention, I began to drift back into time. I drifted back further and further and further, through the decades, centuries, millennia, and eons; all the way back to when there was no life at all on the earth. The earth was barren of all life, and I saw the gases of the earth rise up to meet the gases of the sky; and then it happened.

When the gases of the earth blended with the gases of the sky they formed amino acids, the first building blocks of life (I deduced this many years later), and when these amino acids were formed I felt myself slip into them and *experienced* the genesis of life!

I *knew* that life began the moment I slipped into the blended gases that created the amino acids; and many years later I deduced that the "I" that slipped into the first building blocks of life was Soul, the primordial consciousness of life—but it was the evolved consciousness of my individuated "I" that recognized that it was the primordial un-self-realized "I" of my Soul self that had slipped into the emerging life process!

If this sounds confusing, let me try to simplify it. The "I" that slipped into the emerging life process of the blended gases was my primordial un-self-realized "I", and the "I" that experienced the genesis of life on earth was my reflective Soul self that had taken millions of years of evolution to individuate into a separate identity, or what Keats called "a bliss peculiar to each one by individual existence."

My primordial un-self-realized "I" (un-self-realized Soul consciousness) was the same "I" that went back through time to experience the genesis of life on earth, but my two "I"s were separated by millions of years of evolution; and it is this evolutionary process that I have come to recognize as the evolutionary impulse to individuate the primordial un-self-realized consciousness of life which I deduced to be Soul, the consciousness of God.

This is why I said that we have to *become* to realize who we *are*; but I was not able to reason this out until many years later when I had seven past-life regressions. But before I relate my past-life regression that allowed me to connect the dots and see the Divine Plan of God, let me explain why I wanted to be regressed to my past lives in the first place.

STUPIDITY IS NOT A GIFT OF GOD

Unlike the Buddhist perspective (which Andrew Cohen has embraced) that does not subscribe to the idea of an individual Soul self, I believe that the primordial consciousness of life individuates and gives birth to an individual Soul self; and this Soul self continues to grow and evolve in its own individual identity through the natural process of karma and reincarnation until the natural process of evolution can take it no further, and then, as Gurdjieff said, we have to take evolution into our own hands to realize what Carl Jung's dream teacher so aptly called our "wholeness and singleness of self."

This is why I believe Andrew Cohen has put the carriage in front of the horse with his perspective on the evolutionary process of life; because for the "I" to become aware that it is the a priori *I Am* of the life process (and the universe) it has to *individuate* its own reflective self-identity first. As I said, we have to *become* in order to realize who we *are*!

Soul is who we are, but we will never know this until we individuate our reflective self-consciousness enough to become aware that we are Soul; and this can only be done by taking evolution into our own hands and evolving consciously *into* our true self. In other words, we are not conscious of who we are until we *become* who we are; and **who we are is the individuated consciousness of our divine nature, Soul.**

Ever since I read Jess Stearn's book *The Search for the Soul: Psychic Lives of Taylor Caldwell,* I wanted to know about my past lives. Many years later I got the opportunity, and I was regressed seven times; and in one of my regressions I experienced something that answered the famous three questions asked by the artist Paul Gauguin: 1. *Where do we come from?* 2. *What are we?* 3. *Where are we going?*

Why I wanted to know about my past lives is a long story, which I have revealed in various contexts throughout my writing; but put simply, it was because I had an all-consuming desire to know who I was. Although this is so private it would be prudent to not disclose it, I want to shed light upon man's natural impulse to individuate; so I will relate the experience that compelled me to go on my spiritual quest for my true self.

This happened in my early twenties. For reasons which took me more than forty years to understand, I became "possessed" one night and had a sexual experience that so shocked my conscience that I could not live with myself. Out of shame and guilt I sold my pool hall and vending machine business and fled to France to begin my quest for my true self.

The curious thing about being compelled to do what I did that night was that I knew what I was doing, but I couldn't help myself. I was myself, but I wasn't myself; and the distinction between my two selves was so acute that I vowed to find out who this other "me" was that compelled me to do what I did that night.

Who am I? was a legitimate question for me, then. I simply had to know who I was, because I knew in the depths of my soul that whoever did what he did that night was not the real me; it was me, but not me, and I had to find the real me or die trying. Thus began my spiritual quest through the dark recesses of my own soul for my true self.

When Carl Jung said to Miguel Serrano in *C. G. Jung and Herman Hesse, A Record of Two Friendships*, "the path is very hard," he was speaking from the profound experience of searching for his own lost soul. In *The Red Book*, his private record of what he called his "confrontation with the unconscious," he writes:

"At that time in the fortieth year of my life, I had achieved everything that I had wished for myself. I had achieved honor, power, wealth, knowledge, and every human happiness. Then my desire for the increase of these trappings ceased, the desire ebbed from me and horror came over me. The vision of the flood seized me and I felt the spirit of the depths, but I did not understand him. Yet he drove me on with unbearable inner longing, and I said: 'My soul, where are you? Do you hear me? I speak, I call you—are you there?" (*The Red Book*, A Reader's Edition, p. 127).

Thus began Jung's journey through the underworld of his own unconscious in search of his lost soul (the self that he had compromised for "honor, power, wealth, knowledge, and every human happiness"), and, as he said, the path to find his lost soul was very hard; but he succeeded. This is why he was informed by a dream near the end of his life that he had achieved "wholeness and singleness of self."

That's what my quest for my true self was all about also, to achieve wholeness and singleness of self, which I was fortunate enough to realize; but I would never have found my true self had I not taken the natural impulse to individuate into my own hands and consciously lived the path to wholeness and singleness of self.

Jung concluded with his lifelong study of the individuation process that the impulse to wholeness and singleness of self seems to be the very purpose of life. In *Memories, Dreams, Reflections* he writes: "Unconscious wholeness therefore seems to me the true *spiritus rector* of all biological and psychic events. Here is a principle which strives for total realization—which in man's case signifies the attainment of total consciousness."

But just what is this principle which strives for total realization? This is what one of my past-life regressions answered and why I believe that Andrew Cohen and the Buddhist philosophy of life have put the carriage in front of the horse with their perspective on the Universal Self, which they simply refer to as the *I Am* principle of life.

I don't discount that the Universal Self or *I Am* principle of life exists prior to our realization of it; I firmly believe this also. But I diverge from their perspective that we do not have an independent individual self. From Cohen's and the Buddhist perspective, the Universal Self is our authentic self, and our ego is a false, illusory self. They maintain that ego is just our "sense of self," a mental construct born of our five senses as we experience life; but even if this were true, it does not negate the entire thrust of nature's impulse to individuate the principle which strives for total realization consciousness.

Even if ego is an illusory self, that does not cancel out the possibility of an individuated Soul self, what Keats called "a bliss peculiar to each one by individual existence," and if we could shed light on what this mysterious principle that strives for total realization consciousness is we might bridge the gap that sets the western (Jungian/Gnostic) and eastern (Cohen/Buddhist) philosophies apart; and this is precisely what my fourth past-life regression addresses. If I may then, let me relate why I had seven past-life regressions.

I knew from some of my past-life recollection dreams in my teens that I had lived before, but I need not mention those dreams here; suffice to say that they fueled my desire to know more about my past lives. And then I read Jess Stearn's book on the historical novelist Taylor Caldwell's past lives and I knew that one day I would be regressed to some of my other past lives, which I did many years later when a serendipitous opportunity presented itself.

When the student is ready, the teacher appears says the old saying; and I was ready for my past-life regressions. That's why the divine law of synchronicity offered me an opportunity to explore my past lives; and the life that I wanted to explore first was my previous life, because I suspected that my previous life was responsible for why I felt as I did about my family. I did not fit in with my family, and I wanted to know why.

I learned from my first regression why I did not fit into my family consciousness, but I had karma to work out with my parents and siblings; that's why we reincarnated as a group into one family unit. This regression revealed a great deal about the individuation process of our Soul self, but it wasn't until I had my fourth past-life regression that I connected all the dots and confirmed that we are all sparks of divine consciousness sent into these lower worlds to individuate the consciousness of God through the growth and evolution of our own individual identity.

In short, in my fourth past-life regression I experienced the miracle of the Divine Plan of God, which is to expand the consciousness of God through the evolution of life; and from the perspective of this spiritually enlightening experience I can categorically say that the Cohen/Buddhist belief in the non-existence of the individual self is a misperception of the evolutionary process of life. Here, then, is what I experienced:

I have to mention that this regression came as a total surprise, both to me and my regressionist. In fact it shocked us both. After the preliminary relaxation period, I began to go back through time once again, just like the experience I had many years before when I experienced the genesis of life on earth, only this time I went back even further, all the way back to where I had come from—*right back to the Body of God!*

I was an atom of God blissfully floating in the Great Ocean of Love and Mercy, full of so much love and joy that I cannot express it; but I did not have a sense of self. I had Soul consciousness, but no self-consciousness. I was "an atom of perception," as John Keats saw in his enlightened moment of spiritual awakening.

STUPIDITY IS NOT A GIFT OF GOD

Once again, the "I" that floated in the Great Ocean of Love and Mercy was me, but not yet evolved into a distinct Soul self; and the "I" that experienced myself in the Body of God as an un-self-realized atom of God was my individuated reflective Soul self.

This is difficult to imagine, but not when you experience it; but my regression did not end here. In the same regression I was sent into the lower material worlds where I evolved up the ladder of evolution on earth until I found myself in the body of a higher primate. I was the alpha male of a group of ten or twelve higher primates, and I dominated my group with brute force and power grunts. I realized in my regression that with each power grunt I appropriated the will-to-be from the individuating consciousness of my group—an experience which has enormous ramifications in social behavior; and then it happened: *I experienced the birth of my reflective self-consciousness!*

Up until that moment I had group consciousness, like all species have; but when I gave birth to my reflective self I separated myself from my group consciousness, and from that moment on I began to create personal karma because now I had a sense of self, and thus began the natural karmic individuation process of the a priori *I Am* principle of life!

Finally, the answer to Gauguin's first question *"Where do we come from?"* was answered: we come from the Body of God. And the answer to his second question *"What are we?"* was also answered: we are atoms of God. But to answer the third question *"Where are we going?"* we have to take evolution into our own hands and give birth to our spiritual self-consciousness. This is what Jesus meant by being born again, which I experienced in my mother's kitchen one day while she was kneading bread dough on the kitchen table.

So, from personal experience I *know* that we are all atoms of God sent into these lower worlds to individuate the consciousness of God. We come into life as Soul seeds, if you will, to grow and evolve in our divine nature, which Carl Jung intuited when he wrote: "Unconscious wholeness therefore seems to me the true *spiritus rector* of all biological and psychic events. Here is a principle which strives for total realization—which in man's case signifies the attainment of total consciousness."

This mysterious principle which strives for total realization consciousness is the atom of God, the seed of our Soul self; and nature's impulse to individuate the creative life force is God's desire to grow in the consciousness of God through the life process. This, then, is the other half of the story of the Cohen/Buddhist perspective on "evolutionary enlightenment" and resolves the mystery of the alpha and omega of the self.

We all have an individual self. It is our Soul self that individuates from life to life through the natural process of karma and reincarnation until we are evolved enough to take the natural impulse to individuate into our own hands and evolve consciously into our divine nature, which is the *I Am* principle of life. In short, we have to *become* to realize who we *are*. And this puts the horse where it belongs, in front of the carriage.

The Making of a Novel

Tea with Grace
A Story of Synchronicity and Platonic Love

"Memoir is the facts of life. Fiction is the truth of life."
Alice Munroe
Nobel Laureate, 2013

One day last summer I was in the basement of our new house in Georgian Bay, Ontario going through my boxes of books looking for one of my dream books for research that I was doing for my new book *The Summoning of Noman* when I was strongly nudged to go through my boxes of unpublished manuscripts, and when I came upon my novel "Grace" I read the first few pages and got hocked; so I brought it upstairs to read.

In all honesty, I had completely forgotten that I had written this novel thirteen years ago; so I dubbed it "my forgotten novel." And when I finished reading it I knew I had made the right decision to put it away for all those years, because I was too close to the story to do it the literary justice it deserved; but now it cried out to be heard. So when I brought *The Summoning of Noman* to closure I immediately set to work on "my forgotten novel."

Grace Kendal, a married ex nun from St. John's Newfoundland, moves to St. Jude, Ontario with her husband, who's been awarded the position of principal of St. Jude Separate School, and they hire Oriano Fellicci to paint their new house; but during the course of his work Grace and Oriano connect on a spiritual level and fall in platonic love.

Grace was called to St. Jude, Ontario. She knows that she was called, because she has heard the Call of Soul before; when she was called to the convent; when she was called twenty years later to leave the convent to serve God out in the secular world; and when she was called to motherhood; but she does not understand why she was called to St. Jude, and *Tea with Grace* is the story of why she was called to meet her destiny.

Grace has outgrown her Roman Catholic faith, but she's reluctant to admit it; this is why she was called to St. Jude. Her housepainter, who also happens to be a creative writer, awakens Grace to her spiritual quandary; but the closer she's brought to the edge of her faith with every conversation they have, the more frightened she becomes.

The plot thickens when Grace's daughter Kathleen defies her mother and has an abortion. This pushes Grace to the limits of her faith, and she has a choice to make: accept her daughter for the choice she has made and love her for herself; or hold fast to her faith and fear for her daughter's soul. This is the test that Grace Kendal was called to meet.

Oriano understands her spiritual quandary, and he offers Grace every possible opportunity to expand her faith and liberate herself from the chokehold that it has upon her; but Grace is hesitant to step into the undiscovered country of her anguished soul, and the drama unfolds as she struggles to make sense of her new life in St. Jude.

St. Jude is named after the patron saint of hopeless causes. Ironically, Grace's son Michael has a tragic accident while skiing and becomes a quadriplegic. Grace prays to St. Jude for a miracle cure; but we never know if this is going to happen in real life. However, in the novel that Oriano plans to write based on his relationship with Grace, the spiritual conditions for a miracle cure for Michael are set up; and we can imagine it happening, true to Oriano's aesthetic credo that "art is the miracle of the possible."

Tea with Grace is the story of the making of a novel, and it is the closest we will ever get to the imaginative transformation of reality into a Platonic ideal. It is a story of what is and what could be; a rare glimpse into the mind of a writer that sheds light on the mystical process of creative writing. As the poet Adrienne Rich would say, *Tea with Grace* is "an act of the imagination that transforms reality into a deeper perception of what it is."

An Interview with The Author

Selected Questions and Answers

Q: I got the impression from reading *Stupidity Is Not a Gift of God* that you have a deep sense of personal confidence in your beliefs. I'd like to know where your beliefs come from, because they can be quite convincing.

A: When John Freeman asked Carl Jung if he believed in God in that famous BBC "Face to Face" interview, Jung answered, "I know. I don't need to believe; I know." Jung answered that way because he *knew* from personal experience that God existed. In short, he was at one with his beliefs; and so am I at one with what I believe. That's why I have the confidence of my beliefs. But to answer your question, my beliefs come from an intuitive relationship with life. I've built my life upon the premise that I would rather trust my own truths over anybody else's, which is a very difficult path to take, because you have truths that have been embraced by thousands of people, millions of people over the centuries actually, and when one begins to suspect the truths that these millions of people embrace, and I'm talking about religions like Christianity, Buddhism, scientific realism and different philosophies of life; these truths that these collective bodies of society accept and govern their life by, it's very difficult to stand up to them simply because they don't resonate with how you feel about life. Well, I've had experiences that put me at dissonance with many of these truths. For example, I went to great lengths to understand why there was such dissonance between myself and some of the premises of Christianity; and I made great efforts to find out why. I was a conscious seeker. I did not just formulate my views out of thin air. They began as suspicions, as intuitive insights, and then I sought to explore if my insights were valid or not; and fortunately the merciful law of life works in such a way as to assist you in your efforts to find the truth of your own life, and I was assisted by the merciful law of synchronicity many times in my quest, and always at critical junctures. As I explained in *Stupidity Is Not a Gift of God*, I was dissonant with my Roman Catholic faith, and I left Christianity in my youth and went on a long spiritual quest; and ironically I came back to Christ's teaching because I was not dissonant with the essential teaching of Christ's message. I was dissonant with the religion of Christianity which watered down and distorted Christ's teaching. That's what my novel *Tea with Grace* is all about. So my certainty comes from my own intuitive insights into what is true and what is not true, and from my relentless efforts to validate these insights; and then in my efforts to validate my insights I was given experiences that corroborated them. For example, I had seven past-life regressions that confirmed what I suspected that we pre-exist our mortal human body; which Christianity doesn't believe in because Christianity believes that we only live one life. I embraced reincarnation and karma, and by embracing these two principles life began to make much more sense to me. And in like manner, with respect to Buddhism that does not believe we have an individual self, because Buddhists believe in the a priori *I Am* consciousness of life; they believe that there is only one universal Self, and that this Self expresses itself as a continuum of consciousness that flows through the process of life and I believe that we do have an individual self. Buddhists believe that we are all expressions of the *I Am* consciousness of life, and I don't dispute that. I embrace that also. My dissonance with Buddhism came from my intuition of the process of individuation which led me to believe that we have an autonomous self, and that this self reincarnates from lifetime to lifetime, and it grows in consciousness to the point where it becomes aware that it is the *I Am* consciousness of life, as I explained in my essay "On the Evolutionary Impulse to Individuate." So the certainty of my beliefs comes from my gnostic experience of life, from my intuitive understanding of life, and from my indefatigable efforts to validate my intuitions. I've read much of the literature of life, and by that I mean the wisdom literature of the Way that can be found in every culture; and I found corroborating support, such as Socrates, Rumi, John Keats, Wordsworth, St. Paul, Gurdjieff, and many sources. One of my best sources was Carl Gustav Jung, who had an extraordinary insight into the process of how Soul individuates through life. That's why I'm so confident in my beliefs.

STUPIDITY IS NOT A GIFT OF GOD

Q: I have a question about your novel *Tea with Grace*. This story felt very real to me, and it answered a lot of questions about my faith. I'd like to know if this novel was inspired by a real life experience.

A: Every creative writer will tell you that their personal life will somehow find its way into their novels. Alice Munroe, the first Canadian writer to win the Nobel Prize for literature, draws a distinction between memoir and fiction. In an interview with Shelagh Rogers on CBC shortly after being awarded the Nobel Prize said, "memoir is the facts of life, fiction is the truth of life," and I think it was Saul Bellow's son who said, if you want to know anything about my father's life, read his novels; the same with Philip Roth, and John Irving. John Irving said in an interview that a lot of his personal life goes into his novels. He takes experiences from his life and gives them to his imagination, or to the process of the story itself to work out. Let me say something about John Irving here, if I may; because I'm really intrigued by his creative process. Every creative writer has their own unique process. There's some general pattern to the creative process for all writers, but there's a specific personal quality about each writer's creative process, and I learned that John Irving gets the first sentence for every one of his novels. His first sentence just comes to him, and he does not begin writing his novel until his last sentence comes to him. Now can you imagine? Stop and think for a moment how the creative unconscious works. This man gets the very first sentence for his novel, and then he waits, it could be a week, two weeks, a month, or years, and then he gets the last sentence for his novel; and then he begins to work on his novel, to bring it out into the open. Doesn't that tell you that his novel was already written somewhere in his creative unconscious and he has the hard work of bringing it out; of writing it, shaping it, and making it work? Martin Amis confirms this insight. He said in the BBC interview "Hard Talk" that he felt his novels pre-exist before he writes them. This is a very difficult thing to understand. It's very mystical. This is why Joyce compared writers to God, because they are creators of their own world. And so when you ask me the question, did *Tea with Grace* come from my life, did my idea for that story come from my personal experience, I have to say yes, it did; but my creative unconscious worked an experience I had with the woman who inspired my character Grace. It worked that experience with all of my other life experiences in my creative unconscious and blended them into a story; and then I had to work that story out creatively, and it's a very mystical process. It's very spiritual. And holy, I might add. So my answer to your question has to be a qualified yes. A personal experience inspired my story, but my creative unconscious used everything that I know about life, whatever I had experienced, whatever I had read and learned to create this imagined story of love and denial. But I had a working premise, of course. You can't just go into a novel blind. You have to have a working premise to work with; and my premise was the realization that a person can get trapped by their faith, like my protagonist former Sister of Mercy Grace Kendal. I had her meet the painter/writer Oriano Fellicci, who had the courage to step out of his Roman Catholic faith so he could continue his spiritual growth; or his growth as a person, if you don't want to use the word spiritual, and they get involved in a platonic relationship. A good analogy of Grace Kendal's spiritual dilemma would be a marriage. How many people do you know who got trapped in a marriage and got a divorce because they needed more freedom to grow? There are all kinds of novels and movies about this kind of dilemma, and my working idea was to draw a distinction between Grace Kendal who was trapped by her Roman Catholic faith and Oriano Fellicci who had extricated himself from that same faith and put them together in a situation and then let my creative unconscious work out the dialectic of their relationship, and the end result was a story of synchronicity and platonic love. In all honesty, I had no idea where my story was going because a novel creates its own reality and gives birth to its own truth, but I trust my creative process no less than John Irving trusts his. And if you really want to know how I feel about truth in fiction, I've come to believe that fiction gives the novelist much more latitude to be honest about the human condition, because he can explore human nature in a novel in a way that he could never talk about openly; that's why Saul Bellow said that his most private self was his writing self. "Fiction is no more than the highest form of autobiography," he said. His fiction was the essential truth of his life; and so is mine. And this, I might add, is what defines literary fiction. Popular fiction reflects the human condition with all the attendant drama to engage the reader's interest; but literary fiction transcends the human condition. That's why Karen Blixen said that ***"art is the truth above the facts of life."*** I hope that answers your question.

Q: I have a question about synchronicity, which is a hot topic today. You say that synchronicity is brought about by what you call the omniscient guiding force of life, which you say is Divine Spirit; can you expand on that for me, please?

A: Yes, certainly. And you're right; it is a hot top today. David Wilcock's new book *The Synchronicity Key* goes a long way to expanding the paradigm on synchronicity; but my insight into the providential nature of synchronicity was brought about by one extraordinary meaningful coincidence that I experienced, which I mentioned in my third volume of spiritual musings. In *Stupidity Is Not a Gift of God* I talk about the synchronicity of finding a building lot on a street with my name. If I wouldn't have asked God to give me a sign where to build our new house, I wouldn't have made that connection and attributed the synchronicity to God; but I did deliberately ask God to please give me a sign which lot to buy. And I didn't want just any sign. I said to God: don't bother with me if you're not going to give me an unequivocal sign. Now I have reasons for being so abrupt with God, because my back was to the wall. I had just published a book (*What Would I Say Today If I Were to Die Tomorrow?*) that really upset my community, and it upset my life partner Penny's co-workers at the hospital where she worked; they were making life very difficult for her, and we decided to relocate because it would have made life easier for both of us and eased the tension in the community because we wouldn't be there. So I asked God to please give me a sign which lot to buy, because we were planning to build a new house down in the Georgian Bay area where we had gone for a summer holiday. Actually we were looking online in the Bruce County area as well; but nonetheless, to make a long story short, I ended up buying a building lot in Bluewater, Tiny Township on a street called STOCCO CIRCLE. STOCCO is my surname, CIRCLE is an O, and O is my nickname; so here you definitely have an unequivocal sign. Now, this synchronicity gets better. There happened to be only one lot for sale on STOCCO CIRCLE, and it had just gone up for sale the day that I asked God for a sign. Circumstances were such that the realtor who was supposed to put up the sign on that lot got waylaid, and for whatever mysterious reason never got to put her realtor sign on my property until the day that I drove down to look for a building lot, the same day that I asked God for a sign. That was Saturday. It was a long drive to Georgian Bay, so I stayed overnight in Sault St. Marie and drove into Georgian Bay Sunday, and Monday I was the first person to see the lot; so there were no other inquiries about that piece of property, and it ended up being exactly within our budget range. In fact, it was five thousand dollars below our allotted budget. And so I said to myself, this goes beyond synchronicity; this goes beyond mere meaningful coincidence; this steps over into providential design, into the miraculous realm of divine intervention; and that's when I began to look at synchronicity differently. I began to see that meaningful coincidences are an act of divine providence, or what I simply call the Way. I've experienced the Way so often in my life that I simply call it the omniscient guiding force of life, and it's these kinds of experiences that confirm for me that there is a divine intelligence to life which guides us through life whenever we're in need of guidance. If we interrupt the flow of our life by choices we've made, like the novel I wrote that shocked my community's shadow and set my hometown against me, then this omniscient guiding force of life steps in and gives us experiences that allow us to get on with our personal destiny, experiences like finding a building lot on a street with my name which told me that I was in the right place at the right time in my life. So my reason for believing synchronicity to be more than chance occurrence—there may be some law of physics that brings it about, I don't know; but however it comes about, however a meaningful coincidence comes about, I'm convinced beyond a shadow of a doubt that coincidences are one of the ways that the divine intelligence of God speaks to us and assists us in our journey through life, and until someone proves me differently I'm going to rest my case on that and continue to live my life with that understanding. There's a much deeper meaning to this miraculous coincidence, but I'm reserving that for a novel I hope to write one day. My Muse has already given me the title: "We May be Tiny, but we're not Small." I love that title and can't wait to write it. Does that answer your question?

Q: In your book *Stupidity Is Not a Gift of God* you wrote that meditation is a betrayal of the self. I find that hard to swallow, and I'd like you to expand on that if you would. I've been practicing meditation for twenty years, and what you wrote bothers me.

A: So, it bothers you? Okay. That's good. It got you thinking. I can expand upon my view by simply saying that in the specific context of the Buddhist belief that we don't have an individual self, meditation would be a betrayal of the natural process of individuation. As a means of relaxing the mind, regenerating oneself, and expanding one's consciousness certainly meditation is effective; my only objection is in my understanding that meditation in Buddhism is used to detach oneself from the ego. I suppose there's nothing wrong in detaching oneself from the ego as long as one realizes that the ego can never be negated, because you cannot deny the ego by detaching yourself from it. You cannot negate your ego self, because your ego is your identity in the matrix of your human personality. It is who you are in your current lifetime, and it has to be individuated for you to realize your true self. And my understanding of the individuation process essentially has to do with my gnostic knowledge that to realize the totality of your identity from all of your lifetimes you have to transform and refine the consciousness of your ego self so you can become aware of your total individuality which is born of all your past lives. **"There is no other time or place to find yourself. Now is your only context,"** said Jesus, in Glenda Green's book *Love without End, Jesus Speaks*; so it's not so much that I feel that meditation is a betrayal of the individuation process, as such; only within the specific context of the Buddhist belief that we don't have an independent, autonomous self. Otherwise meditation is a fine way to regenerate oneself and remove oneself from the hurriedness of life and expand one's consciousness; but I personally believe that it is foolish to use meditation to detach oneself from one's ego specifically for the sake of negating one's ego, which seems to be a Buddhist pursuit, because you can't nullify your ego self. You simply cannot. Carl Jung supported this perspective. That's why he never embraced the Buddhist perspective on ego, because his whole psychology has to do with individuating the self, of integrating our unconscious self with our conscious self. The Archetypal Self, which is the *I Am* consciousness of life is forever seeking to be individuated, so it goes contrary to nature to negate the ego self. As incredible as this may sound, **the whole teleological thrust of nature, and the entire Cosmos for that matter, is to individuate the I Am consciousness of God so the I Am consciousness of God can become aware of itself through the individual self of man**. "God is not blessed in his Godhead. He must be born in man forever," said the mystic Meister Eckhart. That's the whole story of the alpha and omega of the Self. The Buddhist teaching says that *I Am* consciousness is all there is, and it somehow takes the individuation process to be already realized in *I Am* consciousness; but even though it may all be one state of coextensive consciousness in the Eternal Now, or in the "all-at-once," as the Australian aborigines call the Eternal Now of Dreamtime, we nonetheless have to go through the *becoming* process; we have to go through the whole stage of growth into the realization that we are one Self, that we are the *I Am* consciousness of life. An acorn seed cannot say, I am an oak tree. An acorn seed is an oak tree *in potentia*, and it has to go through the stages of its own growth to become an oak tree; and so are we the *I Am* consciousness of life insomuch that we are evolving into the realization that we are *I Am* consciousness. We are a Soul seed of our own individual self, if you will; which I validated when I had my seven past-life regressions. This is why I say that Buddhists are putting the carriage in front of the horse. Andrew Cohen is doing the same with his book *Evolutionary Enlightenment*, and I think that does damage to the individuation process. I think that retards spiritual growth instead of enhancing it, as he claims with his new path to spiritual awakening. This perspective keeps you trapped in the Mental Plane of Consciousness, and you will never break through to the Soul Plane and realize your Soul self. As much as I hate to say this, I think the Buddhist perspective gives a person license to be lazy in his understanding in how to transform the consciousness of their ego self. You can't just go into meditation and negate your ego self. If you're going to meditate, the important thing is not to isolate meditation from the rest of your life. You have to allow meditation to transform your actions so you can transcend yourself. That's what I mean by self-betrayal. You can't short-circuit the process of self-individuation by negating your ego self through meditation to realize *I Am* consciousness, just as Christians can't short-circuit the process of spiritual rebirth by embracing Jesus Christ as their savior; you have to go through the life process of transforming the ego self so you can become aware of your Soul self, which is what Jesus Christ's true teaching of spiritual rebirth is all about; and Gurdjieff's teaching. And it's what Jung's psychology of individuation is all about. And the Gnostics were all about this same secret teaching of self-transformation; and the alchemists; and the Sufis; and the Taoists; and Socrates, who also taught the secret science of Soul gathering and collecting herself into herself. We must complete what nature left unfinished. This is the secret of the Golden Flower. This is the mystical union of the inner and outer self of man. This is the sacred marriage of the esoteric mystery schools. Like Eckhart said, "God must be born in man forever." I lived the secret teaching of the Way, and I transcended myself. I transcended the Mental Plane and realized my true self on the Soul Plane of Consciousness. That's how I could say, **"*I am what I am not, and I am not what I am; I am both, but neither: I am Soul.*"** So I don't know how the Buddhists got fixed in their perspective that we only have one self; I really don't. There's something sinister about this belief, because we cannot go through life without an ego self. Ego is our un-self-realized Soul self, and it is not illusory; it is who we are becoming. ***Ego is our Soul self in potentia.*** Ego is to the individuation process what water (consciousness) is to fish (our Soul self), and we cannot *become* who we already are without our ego self. This is the paradoxical nature of our Soul self that the Buddhists haven't been quite able to resolve; but this is precisely what Jesus meant when he said that the two must be made one. This is what the individuation process of the *I Am* consciousness of God is all about. But like Carl Jung said, the path is very hard; because it takes a lot to transform our selfish ego self which has a natural tendency to bloat itself up and grow in its own self-importance. As offensive as this may be to some people, especially Buddhists who believe that ego is an illusory sense of self, I've come to the realization that vanity is a prerequisite for spiritual growth; that's why I appreciate people with large egos now. I just say to myself whenever I see someone with a large ego: boy, they sure have a lot of material to work with on their journey through life, because I know that they're going to be spiritual giants one day—like Saul of Tarsus, for example. The sad part about this however is that it often takes a great tragedy of some sort, or a humiliating fall from grace to get the person to realize the karmic limitations of their inflated ego. But as the proverb says, pride goes before the fall. Well, this happens all the time. The inherently corrective nature of the individuation process shocks one's psyche and liberates Soul from one's egoic limitations. If you follow the career of people in public life, especially in the entertainment business or people in positions of power, you'll notice many examples of people falling from grace; very proud and arrogant people who fall from the giddy heights of their own self-importance. That's just the corrective principle of life at work, because **karma is the inherently self-correcting principle of the individuation process.** This principle will get you back on track eventually, if not in this lifetime the next; so people with large egos are just collecting material—the life force, or Soul consciousness if you will—so they can grow spiritually, because that's how the natural impulse to individuate works, which is why vanity is a prerequisite for spiritual growth. And in all honesty, I enjoy following the career of people with large egos now, because I wait patiently for the fall that's inevitably going to come. Like I said, the individuation process is inherently self-correcting, and no one can cheat their own karma. *"Be not deceived; God is not mocked; for whatsoever a man soweth, that shall he also reap,"* said St. Paul, who himself was spiritually transformed with Christ's teaching of spiritual rebirth. But we're much too spiritually obtuse to see the tragic flaws of our own character; that's what makes life so difficult. And humorous, I might add. It's like St. Padre Pio said in one of my spiritual healing sessions. He likened life unto a joke, but he said the problem is that we won't get the punch line until we get to the other side. Well, it's a lot funnier when you get the punch line on this side because it gives one's appreciation for how life works a kind of sweetness that you wouldn't get over there. On the other side you have the certainty of the knowledge of how life works, but here all you have is an intuitive understanding, and there's a wonderful feeling of sweet satisfaction in that awareness because you've worked it out on your own. *Life really is an experience in self-initiation.* I want to thank you for your thoughtful questions, and may the blessings be.

THE SYMBOL OF THE LOTUS FLOWER

The roots of a lotus are in the mud, the stem grows up through the water, and the heavily scented flower lies pristinely above the water, basking in the sunlight. This pattern of growth signifies the ***progress of the soul*** from the primeval mud of materialism, through the waters of experience, and into the bright sunshine of enlightenment. ***Stupidity Is Not a Gift of God*** is my lotus flower, and my gift to you.

OTHER BOOKS BY OREST STOCCO

Tea with Grace
A Story of Synchronicity and Platonic Love

Letters to Padre Pio

Jesus Wears Dockers,
The Gospel Conspiracy Story

Old Whore Life
Exploring the Shadow Side of Karma

Healing with Padre Pio

Why Bother?
The Riddle of the Good Samaritan

Just Going With the Flow
And Other Spiritual Musings

Keeper of the Flame

My Unborn Child

What Would I Say Today If I Were To Die Tomorrow?
Reflections on the Life of a Seeker

On the Wings of Habitat
A Volunteer's Story

ABOUT THE AUTHOR

Orest Stocco was born in Panettieri, Calabria, Italy. He immigrated to Canada and studied philosophy at university. A student of Gurdjieff's teaching for many years which opened him up to the Way, his passion for writing inspired such works as *Keeper of the Flame* and *Healing with Padre Pio*. He lives in Georgian Bay, Ontario with his life mate Penny Lynn Cates. His personal dictum is: life is an individual journey.
Visit him at: http://www.oreststocco.com
Spiritual Musings Blog:
http://www.spiritualmusingsbyoreststocco.blogspot.com

ME AND MY SISPHYEAN ROCK

www.ingramcontent.com/pod-product-compliance
Lightning Source LLC
Chambersburg PA
CBHW020852090426
42736CB00008B/348